photography by
JONATHAN GREGSON

WILL TORRENT

pâtisserie

Master the art of French pastry at home with this ultimate step-by-step guide

foreword by
HESTON BLUMENTHAL

'From being a very keen, and I mean very keen, young student to becoming a very professional pastry chef I have watched Will's progress with great interest. Now, Will is the teacher and this book allows all of us to look like professionals at home. A great book from an energetic, accomplished and skilled craftsman – you can't help but enjoy it!' BRIAN TURNER

RYLAND PETERS & SMALL

DEDICATION

To my Grandad and my Nans for being my inspiration; for Mum, Dad and Sophie for supporting and believing in me. x

Senior Designer Megan Smith
Commissioning Editor Céline Hughes
Production Manager Gordana Simakovic
Head of Production Patricia Harrington
Art Director Leslie Harrington
Editorial Director Julia Charles

Prop Stylist Liz Belton
Food Stylist Will Torrent
Food Stylist's Assistants Rosie Reynolds, Emily Kydd, Kathryn Morrissey, Alistair Birt
Indexer Hilary Bird

This edition published in 2026
by Ryland Peters & Small
20–21 Jockey's Fields,
London WC1R 4BW

www.rylandpeters.com
Email: euregulations@rylandpeters.com

First published in 2013 as *Pâtisserie at Home* and reissued in 2020.

10 9 8 7 6 5 4 3 2 1

ISBN: 978-1-78879-775-7

Printed and bound in China

A CIP record for this book is available from the British Library.

US Library of Congress Cataloging-in-Publication Data has been applied for.

The authorised representative in the EEA is Authorised Rep Compliance Ltd., Ground Floor. 71 Lower Baggot Street, Dublin, D01 P593, Ireland
www.arccompliance.com

PICTURE CREDITS

All photography by Jonathan Gregson apart from:
p10 Richard Nebesky/Getty Images
p34 Frank Wing/Getty Images
p60 Terry Vine/Getty Images
p86 Jeffrey Becom/Getty Images
p122 Gueorgui Pinkhassov/Magnum Photos
p154 Anton Dijkgraaf/taverneagency.com

NOTES

- All spoon measurements are level, unless otherwise specified.
- Recipes containing raw or partially cooked egg should not be served to the very young, very old, anyone with a compromised immune system or pregnant women.
- Unless otherwise stated, all butter is unsalted, eggs are UK medium or US large, and sugar is caster (UK) or granulated (US).
- Chocolate described as 'dark' for the UK is 'bittersweet' for the US.
- When a recipe calls for the grated zest of citrus fruit, buy unwaxed fruit and wash well before use. If you can only find treated fruit, scrub well in warm soapy water and rinse before using.
- Recipes in this book were tested using a fan-assisted oven. If using a regular oven, follow the manufacturer's instructions for adjusting temperatures. However, as a general rule, temperatures should be increased by about 15–20°C (35°F) if using a regular oven.

MIX
Paper | Supporting responsible forestry
FSC® C106563

Contents

Foreword

I first met Will about ten years ago, when he was fifteen and came to do a week's work experience at the Fat Duck. Even then it was clear he had an old head on young shoulders: he was determined, thoughtful about food and showed a really good understanding of the necessary technical skills.

Somehow, a week working at the Fat Duck didn't put him off cooking, and he's gone from strength to strength, becoming the first British pastry chef to win a Medallion of Excellence at the WorldSkills competition in 2007, gaining the Craft Guild of Chefs Young Chef of the Year award a couple of years later, and a prestigious Acorn Scholarship in 2010. Will has said that his week at the Fat Duck changed his life, so I've followed his career with a certain amount of pride. I was delighted to discover that he had become a pastry chef and pâtisserie development consultant for Waitrose, which means that, a decade on, things have come full circle and we are working together again. Among other things, he now has the unenviable job of developing some of my projects for the company.

Will's the perfect person to do this, because he's curious, imaginative, adaptable and a great technical craftsman. Like me, he likes to push boundaries and do things differently, and he's a bit of an obsessive. (He has those 3am moments where he wakes up and scribbles down some idea that's come to him in his sleep.) Despite all his achievements he has kept his feet on the ground and remained admirably committed to sharing what he knows and encouraging others. These traits make him exactly the sort of guide you need to navigate the intricacies of pastry-making. His book, I'm sure, will become an instant classic. It explains with great clarity all the basics, from puff and choux pastry to crème chantilly and ganache. It covers dozens of the mouthwatering classics of the dessert world – rum baba, millefeuille, tarte au chocolat and tarte au citron, tuiles, madeleines, meringues, Black Forest gâteau, sachertorte, macarons. And there are plenty of twists among these pages to keep you on your toes, fire up your culinary imagination and impress the hell out of whoever's lucky enough to come round for dinner.

Heston Blumenthal

Introduction

When I was growing up, I was surrounded by food, baking, sweets and family.

My Grandad trained as a chef and practised his trade in some of the most famous hotels and restaurants in the seaside town of Bournemouth. What's more, his uncle owned a pâtisserie in Paris (see right) so all this cooking and pastry really is in the blood. My Nans also baked the most amazing cakes – chocolate, fruit and Welsh cakes – so from an early age I understood how food can bring families together and enjoyment to the table when hard work and effort go into a meal. Nans' Welsh cakes were brought home with giddy anticipation – beautiful crumbly little things full of sugar, butter and raisins. Just writing this, I can smell them baking in the kitchen and then hear the unwrapping of the foil and greaseproof paper they were wrapped in.

I have three very vivid memories from my childhood that conjure up nostalgic tastes, aromas and wonderful memories. The first is of making peppermint creams with my friends at infant school and being stunned at the strength of minty flavour. The second is of baking chocolate fudge cake with my Nans for many a birthday celebration – I couldn't quite reach the worktop but I did my best to get stuck in and of course I ate the raw cake mixture from the sides of the bowl and the spoon. We always looked forward to that much more than the traditionally iced fruitcake that Mum always asked for. The third is of a Greek salad made by my Grandad. I must have been about nine or ten years old and I had never tasted feta cheese before! I had always loved cheese on toast but this sour, salty cheese with its unusual texture and smell, chopped in a salad with tomatoes, cucumber and olives, really fed my imagination and I soon caught the cooking bug. With that kind of heritage, it's no wonder I ended up training to be a pastry chef.

Since then, I've been lucky enough to work with some great pastry chefs and in some amazing places, so I hope some of the tips and tricks I've picked up here and there will make your life easier when you set out on your French pâtisserie journey.

French pastry is so often thought of as impossible to achieve at home, and something that only professional pastry chefs with years of training can perfect. Even some of the simpler French desserts have the fear factor for many people out there. But with the growing popularity of baking over recent years, it's time to step into a pastry chef's shoes, attempt some of the classics and surprise yourself. I hope that with my step-by-step guidelines and modern flavour combinations and finishes, you will have the confidence to attempt some of my French pâtisserie, made easy! Keep it familiar but make it new!

Will Torrent

BOULANGERIE
RICHES
GLUTEN
BOURBONNEUX
SES MACARONS
PATISSERIE BOULANGE
BOULANGERIE

Pâtisserie is all about technique, precision and elegance. You only need to look in a Parisian pâtisserie window to appreciate how skilled a pastry chef needs to be to produce identical rows of éclairs, perfectly piped macarons and batch after batch of silken ganache to enrobe petits fours. When you make the decision to replicate these creations at home, you needn't doubt your skills; every basic technique is simple to master if you take your time, are meticulous and don't berate yourself too much for a novice attempt. All these stock pastry doughs, creams and finishing touches are achievable and will provide you with the foundations for so many French pastries.

Basic techniques

Pâte sablée

This is one of my favourite types of pastry. It's a rich, sweet shortcrust but made with icing/ confectioners' sugar to achieve a really lovely crisp, crumbly texture ('sablée' means sandy) that works perfectly with rich cream and fresh fruit. It's so versatile that you can use it for tarts and biscuits but also as the base for gâteaux.

200 g/14 tablespoons butter, softened
100 g/¾ cup icing/ confectioners' sugar
a pinch of salt
1 vanilla bean
finely grated zest of 1 lemon
2 eggs, lightly beaten
250 g/2 cups plain/ all-purpose flour

Makes enough to line a 20-cm/8-in. tart pan

Beat the butter, sugar and salt together in a stand mixer or in a bowl with an electric whisk until pale – about 5 minutes.

Split the vanilla bean lengthwise using a small, sharp knife and scrape the seeds out into the creamed butter mixture. Add the lemon zest and beat again to incorporate.

With the whisk running, gradually add the eggs, mixing until fully incorporated.

Gently mix in the flour but do not over-work the dough otherwise the gluten will develop and you will end up with pastry that is tough rather than crisp and light.

Bring the dough together into a ball with your hands, wrap in clingfilm/plastic wrap and refrigerate until needed – at least 2 hours, but overnight if possible.

Pâte sucrée

This is similar to the pâte sablée but the use of caster/granulated sugar instead of icing/ confectioners' sugar makes a less delicate pastry. Use it to make tarts and as the base for gâteaux.

100 g/7 tablespoons butter, softened
100 g/1 cup sugar
1 vanilla bean
finely grated zest of 1 lemon
2 eggs, lightly beaten
250 g/2 cups plain/ all-purpose flour

Makes enough to line a 20-cm/8-in. tart pan

Beat the butter and sugar together in a stand mixer or in a bowl with an electric whisk until pale – about 5 minutes.

Split the vanilla bean lengthwise using a small, sharp knife and scrape the seeds out into the creamed butter mixture. Add the lemon zest and beat again to incorporate.

With the whisk running, gradually add the eggs, mixing until fully incorporated.

Gently mix in the flour but do not over-work the dough otherwise the gluten will develop and you will end up with pastry that is tough rather than crisp and light.

Bring the dough together into a ball with your hands, wrap in clingfilm/plastic wrap and refrigerate until needed – at least 2 hours, but overnight if possible.

Pâte à sablé Breton

This is a pastry that works so well left on its own and stamped out to make crumbly, buttery biscuits. In the Brittany region of France, it is made into a whole, simple cake or individual biscuits, glazed with egg yolk and scored with a criss-cross pattern. The pastry also marries successfully with other components, such as in the Tarte Croustillante aux Abricots on page 83.

70 g/5 tablespoons butter, softened
60 g/5 tablespoons sugar
1½ egg yolks
100 g/¾ cup plain/all-purpose flour
a pinch of baking powder
a pinch of salt
finely grated zest of 1 lemon
finely grated zest of 1 orange

several ovenproof cookie cutters plus a baking sheet lined with greaseproof paper, or a deep, 18-cm/7-in. tart pan

Makes enough to line a deep, 18-cm/7-in. tart pan

Beat the butter and sugar together in a stand mixer or in a bowl with an electric whisk until pale – about 5 minutes.

With the whisk running, gradually add the egg yolks, mixing until fully incorporated.

Gently fold in the flour, baking powder, salt and citrus zest until fully incorporated. The dough will be very buttery and wet.

Bring the dough together into a ball with your hands. To roll it out, place it between 2 sheets of greaseproof paper and use a rolling pin to flatten the dough until about 2 cm/¾ inch thick. Refrigerate overnight, still between the sheets of paper.

The next day, preheat the oven to 180°C (350°F) Gas 4.

If you are making biscuits, stamp out rounds from the chilled dough with the cookie cutters. Transfer each round, still in the cookie cutter, onto the prepared baking sheet. You need to cook the biscuits inside the cutters because the high butter content makes them spread during baking.

Bake the biscuits in the preheated oven for 20 minutes or until they are wonderfully golden brown, coming away from the cutters and sinking ever so slightly in the middle.

Allow the biscuits to cool completely on the baking sheet and inside the cookie cutters.

Keep in an airtight container before using.

A

B

C

Pâte feuilletée

Pâte feuilletée, or puff pastry, is quite hard to make but try it at least once! It is 'laminated' with lots of butter, which is worked into the pastry and needs several 'turns' to blend it in – this is what makes the magical, crisp layers.

Laminating
500 g/4½ sticks butter, softened
a pinch of salt
100 g/¾ cup strong white bread flour

Dough
2 teaspoons salt
220 ml/1 scant cup water, chilled
juice of ½ lemon
50 g/3 tablespoons butter, softened
120 g/1 cup plain/all-purpose flour
280 g/2 cups strong white bread flour

Makes about 1.2 kg/2½ lbs.

For laminating

Put the butter, salt and flour in a bowl and knead together with your hands to incorporate everything. Turn the mixture out onto a lightly floured surface and flatten it until smooth and about 5 mm/¼ inch thick. Trim the edges with a spatula to get a neat square. **(A)**

Refrigerate for about 1 hour to harden.

For the dough

Put the salt, water and lemon juice in a measuring jug/cup and stir to dissolve the salt.

Either in a mixing bowl with your fingers, or in a stand mixer with a dough hook, mix the butter and flours together until they get crumbly. Gradually pour in the liquid from the measuring jug/cup and mix until a dough forms. **(B)**

On a lightly floured surface or in the stand mixer, knead the dough for 4 minutes. Shape into a ball and refrigerate for 30 minutes.

Remove the chilled dough and butter block from the fridge. Using a rolling pin, roll the dough out to a rectangle 20 x 30 cm/8 x 12 inches. Cut the butter block down the middle and place one half in the middle of the pastry rectangle. Bring one side of the pastry up and over the butter to cover it. Stretch the pastry if needed. Place the second butter block on top of that and fold the remaining flap of pastry over. **(C)**

Roll the dough out into a rectangle again. With a short side in front of you, fold the top third over, then the bottom third on top of that. Now turn the dough 90° clockwise so that the fold is on the left hand side. This process of flattening and folding the dough is called a 'turn'. Poke a hole in the dough to indicate that 1 turn has been made. Refrigerate for 20 minutes.

Give the dough 5 further turns, resting it in the fridge for 20 minutes between each turn and prodding with further holes. **(D)**

Refrigerate for 1 hour before using.

D

A

B

C

Pâte à choux

People often say that they find it really hard to make choux pastry – pâte à choux – but I think it's one of the easiest. As versatile as many classic French pastry doughs, it can be piped into buns and filled with lovely vanilla crème pâtissière in a croquembouche – the classic French wedding cake – or mixed with grated Parmesan, parsley and ham before being deep fried to make wonderful beignets for a summer canapé party.

125 ml/½ cup water
125 ml/½ cup milk
100 g/6½ tablespoons butter
a pinch of salt
a pinch of sugar
140 g/1 cup plus 1½ tablespoons plain/all-purpose flour
approximately 6 eggs

large piping bag fitted with a small, plain nozzle/tip (optional)
baking sheet, lined with greaseproof paper

Makes 12–16 small buns

Preheat the oven to 180°C (350°F) Gas 4.

Put the water, milk, butter, salt and sugar in a medium saucepan over medium heat. Stir constantly with a silicone or wooden spoon so that the sugar doesn't burn and cause the mixture to stick to the bottom of the pan.

When it comes to the boil, quickly stir in the flour and mix together. Beat the dough vigorously until it cleanly leaves the sides of the saucepan – this can take up to 5 minutes, depending on the heat. **(A)**

Transfer the dough to a stand mixer or mixing bowl (using an electric whisk) and beat in the eggs, one at a time. You might not need all 6 eggs – flour and eggs behave differently no matter how many times you make the same recipe, so the number of eggs needed can vary. **(B)**

As you add the eggs and beat them in, watch the dough and when it is soft and smooth and drops off a spoon leaving behind a 'V' shape, it is ready. **(C)**

To make choux buns, spoon the dough into the prepared piping bag. Pipe bulbs onto the prepared baking sheet, about 5 cm/2 inches in diameter and spaced apart as they will expand during baking. **(D)**

Bake in the preheated oven for 10–15 minutes, depending on the size of the buns. They should be golden brown and hollow in the middle.

D

A

B

C

D

Croissant pastry

The humble croissant is one of the most delicious foodie joys around. Freshly baked, torn apart, eaten with creamy salted butter, rich, fruity jam and a cup of strong coffee in Paris – nothing much beats that. I always have croissants in the freezer ready to go and although the method is quite challenging, once you get the hang of it, they are so easy to make. Perfect for special breakfasts, using in desserts or just for a lazy Sunday morning with the papers!

Laminating

300 g/2½ sticks butter, room temperature
40 g/⅓ cup plain/ all-purpose flour

Dough

30 g/2 cakes fresh yeast or 15 g/3 teaspoons dried yeast
230 ml/1 scant cup cold milk
2½ tablespoons sugar
2 teaspoons honey
380 g/3 cups strong white bread flour
2 teaspoons salt
egg yolk mixed with a pinch of salt, to glaze

Makes about 14

For laminating

Put the butter and flour in a bowl and knead together with your hands to incorporate them. Turn the mixture out onto a sheet of clingfilm/ plastic wrap, top with another sheet and flatten with a rolling pin into a rough square about 10 cm/4 inches across. **(A)**

Refrigerate for about 1 hour to harden.

For the dough

Put the yeast and milk in a bowl and stir until the yeast has dissolved. Add the sugar and honey and stir again.

Either in a mixing bowl with your fingers, or in a stand mixer with a dough hook, mix the flour and salt together, then pour in the yeast mixture. Mix slowly until the mixture comes together into a dough.

On a lightly floured surface or in the stand mixer, knead the dough for 10 minutes.

If using a mixer, turn the dough out onto a lightly floured surface and cover lightly with the butter wrapper or a sheet of parchment paper. Allow to rest for 10 minutes.

After 10 minutes, using a rolling pin, roll the dough out to a rectangle about 20 x 30 cm/ 8 x 12 inches. Remove the butter block from the fridge and cut it down the middle. Place one half in the middle of the pastry rectangle. Bring one side of the pastry up and over the butter to cover it. Stretch the pastry if needed. Place the second butter block on top of that and fold the remaining flap of pastry over. **(B)**

Roll the dough out into a rectangle again. With a short side in front of you, fold the top third over, then the bottom third on top of that. Now turn the dough 90° clockwise so that the fold is on the left hand side. This process of flattening and folding the dough is called a 'turn'. Poke a hole in the dough to indicate that 1 turn has been made. Refrigerate for 30 minutes.

Give the dough another turn and allow to rest for 30 minutes. **(C)**

Give the dough a third turn and allow to rest for 2 hours.

At this stage, you can choose to make croissants as described here, or opt for one of the variations on page 171.

After 2 hours, to make croissants, roll the dough out on a lightly floured surface into a rectangle about 3 mm/⅛ inch thick.

Cut the dough in half lengthwise using a large, sharp knife. You now have 2 strips. Trim the edges if necessary to make sure the strips are neat rectangles.

E

F

Put the long side of 1 strip in front of you. Cut out isosceles triangles (tall, with 2 equal sides) measuring about 8 cm/ 3½ inches across the base, all along the strip. They will naturally alternate in direction along the strip. **(D)**

A little tip I once heard in France was that if you cut a snip in the centre of the base of each triangle, you will get a lovely turn at the tips of the croissant. So, using a knife or a pair of scissors, make a snip in the centre of each base.

Starting from the base, roll up each triangle to make a croissant. **(E)**

At this point, you can freeze the croissants for another time. Take them out of the freezer the night before you want to bake them and place them on a baking sheet. Cover them loosely with a tea towel and they will be defrosted, risen and ready to bake by the following morning.

Place the croissants on a baking sheet lightly dusted with flour. **(F)**

Loosely cover the croissants with lightly oiled clingfilm/plastic wrap and allow to rise in a warm place until they have nearly doubled in size – about 2 hours.

About 15 minutes before you are ready to bake, preheat the oven to 200°C (400°F) Gas 6.

Uncover the risen croissants and brush them lightly with the egg wash to glaze.

Bake in the preheated oven for about 12 minutes, or until golden brown and crispy.

Crème pâtissière

This is without question the most luxurious cream on the planet! The basis of so many classic French pastries, this is rich, sweet, smooth and velvety – and simple to make too. My way of making it isn't strictly traditional but it does ensure a thick, stable crème. Once you've mastered the technique, you can experiment with flavourings to adapt it to a particular cake.

1 vanilla bean
500 ml/2 cups milk
100 g/½ cup raw cane sugar
4 egg yolks
25 g/3 tablespoons cornflour/cornstarch
25 g/1½ tablespoons custard powder/ vanilla pudding mix (or additional cornflour/cornstarch)
2 tablespoons butter

Makes about 750 g/ 1½ lbs.

Split the vanilla bean lengthwise using a small, sharp knife and scrape the seeds out into a large saucepan. Drop the bean in too and pour in the milk. Bring to the boil over low heat.

Meanwhile, in a mixing bowl, whisk the sugar, egg yolks, cornflour/cornstarch and custard powder together with a balloon whisk until smooth and creamy.

Pour half the boiled milk into the mixing bowl containing the egg mixture and whisk together. Now pour the contents of the bowl into the saucepan where the remaining milk is. Fish out the vanilla bean with a slotted spoon.

Over low heat, whisk the mixture until it thickens and starts to bubble.

After 5 minutes, the heat will have cooked the cornflour/cornstarch and custard powder and become thick and rich.

Finally, add the butter and whisk it in until melted to further enrich the crème and make it extra glossy.

Transfer the crème pâtissière to a bowl and immediately place a sheet of clingfilm/plastic wrap over the surface to prevent a skin from forming. Allow to cool completely before using.

VARIATIONS

Chocolate: replace the cornflour/cornstarch and custard powder with 3½ teaspoons cornflour/cornstarch, 3 tablespoons plain/all-purpose flour and 3½ teaspoons cocoa powder. Follow the recipe as above, adding the cocoa powder at the same time as the cornflour/cornstarch. At the end, stir in 25 g/1 oz. melted dark chocolate.

Mango and passionfruit: replace the milk with a mixture of mango and passionfruit purées, or a combined mango and passionfruit smoothie.

Praline: add 50 g/¼ cup praline paste (available online) to the milk.

Boozy: stir in 1 tablespoon rum or Grand Marnier at the end.

Apricot: first make an apricot purée. Put 225 g/1½ cups dried apricots, the juice of 2 lemons, 200 ml/¾ cup orange juice and 100 g/½ cup sugar in a saucepan over medium heat and bring to the boil. Lower the heat and simmer for 30 minutes. Allow to cool slightly, then transfer to a blender or food processor and process to a purée. Pass the purée through a sieve/strainer to make it extra smooth. To make the apricot crème pâtissière, replace half the milk with the same amount of apricot purée. Store any remaining purée in an airtight container in the fridge.

Crème diplomate

Sometimes crème pâtissière can be too thick or rich for a delicate dessert pastry, so this cream is perfect. It's crème pâtissière carefully mixed with lightly whipped cream to give a still luxurious, velvety cream but that little bit fluffier.

250 ml/1 cup whipping cream
250 ml/1 cup double/heavy cream
500 g/2 cups storebought crème pâtissière, or 1 x quantity Crème Pâtissière (page 25)

Makes about 1 kg/2¼ lbs.

Put the whipping cream and double/heavy cream in a stand mixer or use a mixing bowl and an electric whisk. Beat until soft, billowing peaks form.

Be careful not to over-whip it otherwise it will become thick and grainy and it will split when mixed in with the crème pâtissière.

Gently fold the whipped cream, in stages, into the crème pâtissière until smooth and irresistible.

Refrigerate until ready to use (or eat straight from the bowl!).

Crème chantilly

Almost everyone's idea of heaven, this is the simplest cream but it gives such joy and harmony to desserts. Spooned lovingly onto summer strawberries with a light grating of orange zest, or served as an accompaniment to a slice of rich, dense chocolate tart to help it go down, you only need four ingredients!

1 vanilla bean
250 ml/1 cup whipping cream
250 ml/1 cup double/heavy cream
50 g/¼ cup caster/superfine sugar

Makes about 550 g/1¼ lbs.

Split the vanilla bean lengthwise using a small, sharp knife and scrape the seeds out into a stand mixer or use a mixing bowl and an electric whisk.

Add the whipping cream, double/heavy cream and sugar and beat until soft, billowing peaks form.

Be careful not to over-whip it otherwise it will become thick and grainy and won't be pleasant to eat – you want this cream to be luxuriously smooth and velvety.

Frangipane

Frangipane is the backbone of so many French pastries and tarts and was one of the first things I learnt how to make when training to become a pastry chef. It's so versatile that it can be used as a filling but equally it can be baked in a little tin, as I do, and eaten as a delicious almond cake with a little jam and a cup of rich coffee.

100 g/6½ tablespoons butter, softened
100 g/½ cup caster/ superfine sugar
3 eggs
100 g/1 cup ground almonds
2½ tablespoons plain/ all-purpose flour

Makes about 400 g/14 oz.

Beat the butter and sugar together in a stand mixer or in a bowl with an electric whisk on high speed for up to 4 minutes. You don't want to get too much air in there otherwise it will puff up in the oven – frangipane should be dense and moist.

Add the eggs, one at a time, and beat until well mixed.

Fold in the ground almonds and flour with a large spoon until evenly incorporated.

The frangipane will keep in an airtight container in the fridge for a few days.

Chocolate and hazelnut frangipane

This takes frangipane to a whole new level and is a particular favourite of mine. I especially like it spiked with spices and spooned into a tart with mulled poached pears on top for a wonderful Christmas dessert.

50 g/1½ oz. dark chocolate, chopped
100 g/6½ tablespoons butter, softened
100 g/½ cup caster/ superfine sugar
4 eggs
25 g/¼ cup ground almonds
75 g/½ cup ground hazelnuts
2½ tablespoons plain/ all-purpose flour

Makes about 450 g/1 lb.

Melt the chocolate on low power in a microwave or in a heatproof bowl over a pan of simmering water (not letting the base of the bowl touch the water).

Beat the butter and sugar together in a stand mixer or in a bowl with an electric whisk on high speed for up to 4 minutes. You don't want to get too much air in there otherwise it will puff up in the oven – frangipane should be dense and moist.

Add the eggs, one at a time, and beat until well mixed.

Fold in the ground almonds, hazelnuts and flour with a large spoon until evenly incorporated.

Finally, fold in the melted chocolate.

The frangipane will keep in an airtight container in the fridge for a few days.

Ganache

There is no doubt that cocoa is one of the world's finest ingredients, discovered by the Aztecs and branded the food of the gods. Chocolate ganache is found in all sorts of guises in French pastry, namely in chocolate truffles. These are sold in pâtisseries and chocolatiers all over France, but more and more chocolatiers around the world are following suit and creating truffles to rival their French counterparts. Follow this method and you will have perfect ganache every time.

100 ml/scant ½ cup whipping cream
a pinch of salt
200 g/7 oz. dark chocolate (70% cocoa), chopped
1 tablespoon butter

Makes about 300 g/10½ oz.

Put the cream in a saucepan and bring to the boil over low heat.

Put the chocolate, salt and butter in a heatproof bowl and pour in the boiled cream. **(A)**

Using a spatula, start to mix the ingredients in a circular motion, just in the centre of the bowl. Keep mixing in a tight circle until the chocolate starts to melt and emulsify with the liquid. **(B)**

Gradually widen the circle to incorporate more of the mixture. **(C)**

When you have reached the edge of the bowl, the chocolate should be entirely melted and all the ingredients should have emulsified and combined into a shiny, rich, velvety truffle ganache. **(D)**

If the ganache looks like it is splitting, add a dash of cold milk – that should bring it back.

Italian meringue buttercream

This buttercream is made using Italian meringue which makes it ultra glossy and decadent.

250 g/1¼ cups caster/superfine sugar
100 ml/6 tablespoons water
5 large egg whites
50 g/¼ cup caster/superfine sugar
500 g/4½ sticks butter, softened and cubed
1 shot of espresso or 50 g/⅓ cup instant coffee granules (optional)

sugar thermometer

Makes about 1 kg/2¼ lbs.

Put the 250 g/1¼ cups sugar and the water in a saucepan and bring to the boil. Simmer over low heat until the syrup reaches 121°C/250°F on a sugar thermometer. Use a brush dipped in cold water to dislodge any sugar crystals on the side of the pan. This will stop the syrup from crystallizing.

Meanwhile, put the egg whites and the 50 g/¼ cup sugar in a stand mixer and begin whisking until stiff peaks form. You can use a heatproof bowl and an electric whisk but you may need a second person's help when you come to pour the syrup in!

Once the syrup has reached the right temperature, slowly pour it in a steady stream into the meringue bowl with the beaters still running. Avoid letting the syrup touch the beaters otherwise you'll get lumps of hardened sugar. Keep whisking until you have used up all the syrup and the meringue is glossy, thick and has cooled substantially – this may take several minutes of whisking. The bowl itself must have cooled too.

Now add the butter, a cube at a time, whisking well between each addition until the butter is used up and fully incorporated in the meringue. Finally, whisk in the coffee, if using.

A

B

C

D

Finishing touches

Caramelized nuts

100 g/⅔ cup shelled pistachios, almonds or hazelnuts
50 g/6 tablespoons icing/ confectioners' sugar
1 tablespoon vodka

Put the nuts, sugar and vodka into a heavy-based saucepan and continually stir over medium heat until the sugar crystallizes around the nuts. Remove from the heat and scatter onto a sheet of greaseproof paper. Allow to cool before using.

Alternatively, allow the nuts to caramelize for longer and add a further 3 tablespoons sugar to the pan.

Chocolate shards

100 g/3½ oz. dark chocolate

sheet of acetate or greaseproof paper

Temper the chocolate following the instructions on the right, or melt it on low power in a microwave or in a heatproof bowl over a pan of simmering water (not letting the base of the bowl touch the water). When it looks like it has all melted, give it a quick stir until smooth. Spread the melted chocolate thinly onto a sheet of acetate or greaseproof paper with a spatula and allow to set.

If you want to transfer a pattern on the chocolate, as on page 64, you can buy transfer sheets especially for chocolate from online cake decorating suppliers.

Chocolate curls

1 bar of chocolate

Remove the chocolate from the packaging and put it upside down on a chopping/cutting board, at the end nearest you. With one hand at each end of a large, sharp knife, and holding it crossways in front of you, carefully bring the blade down onto the bar of chocolate. Start at the end furthest to you and scrape it gently towards you to create curls and shavings.

Tempering chocolate

Tempering chocolate means melting it in a controlled way in order to manipulate the formation of cocoa butter crystals and produce shiny, snappy and crisp chocolate.

You will need a sugar or cooking thermometer (available from good supermarkets) which registers temperatures from as low as 45°C/113°F. This will help you to accurately control the temperature of the chocolate.

There are a few ways of tempering chocolate but I personally recommend the 'seeding' method. Melt two-thirds of your chosen amount of chopped chocolate on low power in a microwave or in a heatproof bowl over a pan of simmering water. Do not let the base of the bowl touch the water and do not let any steam or water get in.

Once the chocolate has melted, dip the thermometer in and it should read 45°C/113°F. If it is higher, allow it to cool down to that temperature. If it is lower, very briefly heat it a little more. When it is the correct temperature, stir in the remaining chocolate. Continue to stir until it reaches 32°C/89.6°F (for dark chocolate), 31°C/87.8°F (for milk) and 29–30°C/84–86°F (for white).

Candied Orange

400 g/2 cups sugar
400 ml/1¾ cups water
2 oranges

Cut the peel off the orange (avoiding the bitter white pith underneath) in large chunks. Then, using a sharp knife, chop the peel into very fine strands. Put one-quarter of the sugar and one-quarter of the water into a saucepan and bring to the boil. Drop the strips of zest into the boiling syrup and boil for 5 minutes. Tip the contents of the pan into a sieve/strainer over the sink and run cold water over it. Put the drained zest back into the pan, add another quarter of the sugar and water and repeat as above, then repeat twice more. The last time, instead of pouring away the syrup, put it in an airtight container with the zest and allow to cool completely.

It will keep, refrigerated, for up to 1 month.

4me ARR
RUE
DES FRANCS
BOURGEOIS
RUE
DE SÉVIGNÉ
23 PATISSERIE

Walk down a high street in France and your eyes will inevitably be drawn towards a beautifully arranged assortment of cakes in a pâtisserie. Peer through the spotless window and you'll see all manner of delights spanning glossy to crumbly via domed, sticky, vibrant, rich, miniature, symmetrical and refined. Sweetened cream, praline, frangipane, meringue, choux pastry and puff pastry are all to be found here, whether in a large celebration cake, or in an individual portion of dessert. Carême is the most famed pâtissier of the nineteenth century and is credited with many of the more elaborate pâtisserie innovations.

Pâtisserie

Framboisiers

There is nothing better than fresh fruit in the summer, and raspberries are my favourite. This simple little cake joins juicy, tart raspberries with luxuriously decadent crème diplomate and soft almond sponge cake. It's mouthwatering! It works with other berries too – in the winter, for example, blackberries (frozen from earlier in the year) with a touch of spice in the cake make a lovely alternative.

Almond cake

120 g/½ cup egg whites (about 4 egg whites)
80 g/scant ½ cup sugar
4 eggs
130 g/1¼ cups ground almonds
75 g/scant ⅔ cup icing/confectioners' sugar
40 g/5 tablespoons plain/all-purpose flour
2 tablespoons butter, melted and cooled
50 g/⅓ cup flaked/slivered almonds

Filling

300 g/2⅓ cups raspberries
1 x quantity Crème Diplomate (page 26)

2 Swiss/jelly roll pans, lined with greaseproof paper
20 x 30-cm/8 x 12-in. rectangle frame

Makes 12

Start the recipe the day before you want to serve the framboisiers.

For the almond cake

Preheat the oven to 190°C (375°F) Gas 5.

Put the egg whites and sugar in a stand mixer or in a bowl using an electric whisk and whisk until stiff peaks form.

Whisk in the whole eggs.

Gently fold in the ground almonds, icing/confectioners' sugar and flour using a large metal spoon.

Finally, stir in the melted butter.

Spoon the mixture into the prepared Swiss/jelly roll pans and spread level with a spatula. Sprinkle the flaked/slivered almonds evenly over the top.

Bake in the preheated oven for 5–10 minutes or until springy to the touch and golden on top. Flip each slab of cake onto a sheet of greaseproof paper dusted with a little semolina. Peel the baking paper off the top and allow the cakes to cool.

For the filling

Fold the raspberries into the Crème Diplomate. If I am making this for children, I love to crush the raspberries first and ripple them through the cream.

Press the rectangle frame down on top of one cooled cake slab in turn to cut out equal rectangles of cake. Leave the frame pressed into one cake and spread the raspberry crème diplomate over the cake layer within the frame. Spread level with a spatula

Place the second cake slab on top (almond-side down) and press down gently with your hand.

Freeze overnight, still in its frame. This will make it easier to cut smoothly.

The next day, gently ease the frame away from the framboisier and cut it into 12 neat fingers using a hot, sharp knife.

Allow to defrost before serving, then dust with icing/confectioners' sugar.

You could also leave the framboisier whole and serve it as a lovely birthday cake.

White chocolate and almond meringue domes

2 tablespoons flaked/ slivered almonds, toasted

Almond meringue discs
50 g/¼ cup egg whites (2–3 egg whites)
juice of ½ lemon
100 g/½ cup sugar
1 teaspoon vanilla extract
2½ tablespoons ground almonds
1½ tablespoons chopped almonds

Amaretto ganache
3½ tablespoons whipping cream
2 tablespoons Amaretto liqueur
125 g/4½ oz. dark chocolate, chopped
2 teaspoons butter

Chocolate mousse
200 g/7 oz. white chocolate, chopped
175 ml/⅔ cup double/ heavy cream
1 egg white

White chocolate ganache
3½ tablespoons whipping cream
150 g/5 oz. white chocolate, chopped

baking sheet, lined with greaseproof paper
6-hole half-sphere silicone pan

Makes 6

These treats are filled with white chocolate mousse, Amaretto ganache and almond meringue, then coated in white chocolate ganache – stunning!

Start the recipe the day before you want to serve the domes.

For the almond meringue discs
Preheat the oven to 110°C (225°F) Gas ¼.

Put the egg whites and lemon juice in a stand mixer or in a bowl using an electric whisk and whisk until frothy.

Add one-third of the sugar to the bowl and whisk until it looks like it has dissolved.

Add another third of the sugar and whisk until the mixture trebles in volume and starts to properly resemble meringue.

Stop the stand mixer or whisk and add the last of the sugar as well as the vanilla to the bowl. On a very high speed, whisk briefly just to incorporate the sugar, then stop immediately. Add the ground and chopped almonds.

Measure the diameter of the holes in the silicone pan. Using a teaspoon, spoon out a little meringue onto the prepared baking sheet and spread it with the back of the spoon to the recorded diameter. Make 6 discs like this.

Bake in the preheated oven for 1 hour, then turn the oven off and allow the meringues to cool completely inside the oven with the door closed. This could ideally be done overnight.

For the Amaretto ganache
Put the cream and Amaretto in a saucepan and bring to the boil over low heat. Pour the boiled cream into a wide, heatproof bowl and add the chocolate and butter. Using a spatula, start to mix the ingredients in a circular motion, just in the centre of the bowl. Keep mixing in a tight circle until the chocolate starts to melt and emulsify with the liquid. Gradually widen the circle until all the chocolate has melted and you have a shiny, smooth ganache.

For the chocolate mousse
Melt the chocolate in a microwave or in a heatproof bowl over a pan of simmering water (not letting the base of the bowl touch the water). Whisk the cream and egg white in separate bowls until soft peaks form. Gently fold the cream and then the egg white into the melted chocolate with a large metal spoon.

Spoon some of the mousse into the holes of the silicone pan. Using the back of the spoon, spread the mousse up the sides of the dome. Spoon the Amaretto ganache into the lined domes and cover with more mousse.

Seal each dome with a meringue disc and press down so that the excess mousse oozes out. Scrape off the excess with a knife and make sure there are no gaps round the meringue. Freeze overnight.

For the white chocolate ganache
The next day, make the white chocolate ganache as described above (it won't have butter).

Gently ease the frozen domes out of the pan and place on a wire rack. Pour the warm ganache over them. It will set very quickly over the frozen domes. Allow to defrost in the fridge. To serve, decorate with flaked/slivered almonds.

A

B

C

Opéras

The opéra, named after the Paris Grand Opéra of the 1900s, comprises neat layers of sponge, buttercream and ganache, all enticingly flavoured with coffee.

Almond Cake mixture (page 36)
5 tablespoons instant coffee granules

Filling and finishing
3 x quantities Ganache (page 30, made with 500 g/1 lb. 2 oz. dark and 100 g/3½ oz. milk chocolate)
2 teaspoons instant coffee granules
8 tablespoons ready-made coffee
1 x quantity coffee Italian Meringue Buttercream (page 30)

3 Swiss/jelly roll pans, lined with greaseproof paper

20 x 30-cm/8 x 12-in. rectangle frame

Makes 12

Start the recipe the day before you want to serve the cake. Preheat the oven to 190°C (375°F) Gas 5.

Make the Almond Cake mixture following the instructions on page 36, but add the instant coffee granules at the same time as the other dry ingredients. Spread the mixture thinly and evenly onto the prepared pans and bake in the preheated oven for 5–10 minutes. Flip each slab of cake onto a sheet of greaseproof paper dusted with a little semolina. Peel the baking paper off the top and allow the cakes to cool.

For the filling and finishing

Make the Ganache following the instructions on page 30, then fold in the coffee granules at the end. Allow to cool slightly.

Press the rectangle frame down on top of each cake slab in turn to cut out equal rectangles of cake. Leave the frame pressed into one cake and brush half the ready-made coffee over the cake within the frame. **(A)**

Spread half the Italian Meringue Buttercream over that and spread level with a spatula. **(B)**

Freeze for 10 minutes to set, then spoon one-quarter of the ganache over the top of the buttercream and spread level. **(C)**

Place a second cake slab on top. Top with the remaining coffee, buttercream and one-quarter of the ganache as before and freeze for 30 minutes to set.

Place the last cake slab on the top and spread another quarter of the ganache over it. Freeze overnight, still in its frame, and reserve the last of the ganache.

The next day, warm the reserved ganache to liquify it. Gently ease the frame away from the layered opéra and cut it into 12 neat fingers using a hot, sharp knife.

Put the slices on a wire rack over a tray and pour the ganache over each one to enrobe it. Allow to set before serving.

Almond and cherry meringues

I remember being wowed by meringues as a kid. I've never forgotten that feeling on a Sunday afternoon in the summer holidays when my mum brought home meringue nests filled with gently whipped cream and fresh fruit; I always scraped off the fruit and cream and just ate the meringues. This recipe is my homage to that childhood memory and it's so simple but brings so much pleasure. You could just as easily pipe delicate little meringues or spoon the mixture into a big pavlova. Here I have created giant meringue clouds marbled with cherry purée and sprinkled with almonds for extra flavour and crunch. They look amazing piled high on a plate for tea.

50 g/¼ cup egg whites (2–3 egg whites)
juice of ½ lemon
100 g/½ cup sugar
1 teaspoon vanilla extract
2 tablespoons Cherry Purée (page 100)
3 tablespoons flaked/slivered almonds
100 g/3½ oz. dark Tempered Chocolate (page 33)

baking sheet, lined with greaseproof paper

Makes about 8

Preheat the oven to 110°C (225°F) Gas ¼.

Put the egg whites and lemon juice into a very clean stand mixer or in a bowl with an electric whisk and whisk until frothy.

Add one-third of the sugar to the bowl and whisk until it looks like it has dissolved.

Add another third of the sugar and whisk until the mixture trebles in volume and starts to properly resemble meringue.

Stop the stand mixer or whisk and add the last of the sugar as well as the vanilla to the bowl. On a very high speed, whisk briefly just to incorporate the sugar, then stop immediately. Although the meringue will look grainy, this adds extra crunch and helps to keep the meringues' volume and shape better.

Pour the cherry purée into the bowl and lightly ripple it through with a knife, just briefly, to create a marbled effect.

Take a large metal spoon and spoon large clouds of meringue onto the prepared baking sheet. Sprinkle almonds over each meringue.

Bake in the preheated oven for 1 hour, then turn the oven off and allow the meringues to cool completely inside the oven with the door closed. This could ideally be done overnight.

When the meringues are cold, dip the bases in Tempered Chocolate to add even more flavour, texture and, of course, indulgence. Allow to set on a wire rack.

A

B

C

Apple and Calvados crumble choux buns

1 x quantity Pâte à Choux (page 18)
1 x quantity Crème Diplomate (page 26)
2 tablespoons Calvados
icing/confectioners' sugar, to dust

Crumble topping
80 g/5 tablespoons butter, softened
100 g/½ cup light brown sugar
100 g/¾ cup plain/ all-purpose flour

Apple compote
500 g/18 oz. Bramley apples
2 tablespoons butter
50 g/¼ cup light brown sugar
juice and grated zest of 1 lemon

baking sheet, lined with greaseproof paper
piping bags, plain nozzle/tip and star-shaped nozzle/tip

Makes 12–16 small buns

These choux buns have a surprise inside (apple compote and Calvados cream) and on top (crumble crust) – delightful in summer or autumn!

For the crumble topping

Beat the butter and sugar together in a stand mixer or in a bowl with an electric whisk just until well combined. Add the flour and bring together into a dough with your hands. Turn the dough out onto a sheet of greaseproof paper, top with another sheet and flatten with a rolling pin until about 3 mm/⅛ inch thick. Freeze for 1 hour.

Preheat the oven to 180°C (350°F) Gas 4.

Make the Pâte à Choux following the instructions on page 18 and pipe into buns on the prepared baking sheet. Take the crumble topping out of the freezer, remove the top sheet of paper and stamp out 2.5-cm/1-inch rounds from the frozen dough – use a cookie cutter or cut around a bottle top. Cut out the same number as there are buns and place a round on top of each bun. **(A)**

Bake in the preheated oven for 15 minutes or until cooked through, puffed up and golden, then turn the oven off and leave the buns inside to cool completely and dry out.

For the apple compote

Peel, core and chop the apples. Put them in a saucepan with the butter, sugar and lemon juice and zest. Cover with a lid and cook over medium heat for 5 minutes. Stir, raise the heat and cook for a further 5 minutes or until you get a chunky 'compote'. Allow to cool completely.

Make the Crème Diplomate following the instructions on page 26, then fold in the Calvados at the end.

Cut each chou bun in half horizontally and spoon some of the compote in the bottom. **(B)**

Fill the piping bag with crème diplomate. Pipe a generous mound on top of the compote. **(C)**

Sandwich with the other half of the bun. Dust with icing/confectioners' sugar, to serve.

Paris-Brest

The classic Paris-Brest was allegedly invented by a Parisian pâtissier in honour of a bicycle race between Paris and Brest in the late 1800s. His incarnation featured two large ring-shaped choux-pastry cakes to resemble bicycle wheels but I have made mine small. It is really up to you. I love the combination of buttery choux pastry, rich praline cream and crunchy roasted hazelnuts so I have opted for these flavours here, but you would normally find flaked/slivered almonds rather than hazelnuts on a Paris-Brest. Personally, I find that the hazelnuts tie in well with the praline.

1 x quantity Pâte à Choux (page 18)
100 g/¾ cup hazelnuts
1 x quantity praline Crème Pâtissière (page 25), chilled
icing/confectioners' sugar, to dust

piping bag fitted with a plain nozzle/tip
2 x 6-hole mini savarin or ring doughnut pans, greased

Makes 12

Preheat the oven to 180°C (350°F) Gas 4.

Put the hazelnuts on a baking sheet and roast in the preheated oven for a few minutes, stirring halfway through, until lightly toasted. Leave the oven on.

Allow the hazelnuts to cool completely, then finely chop half of them and leave the remaining nuts whole.

Make the Pâte à Choux following the instructions on page 18 and pipe into the savarin or ring doughnut pans.

Sprinkle the chopped hazelnuts over the top.

Bake in the hot oven for 10–15 minutes, then turn the oven off and leave the buns inside to cool completely and dry out.

Using a serrated knife, cut each bun in half horizontally. Fill the piping bag with praline Crème Pâtissière and pipe 6–7 bulbs of cream on the cut side of the bottom halves of the buns. Leave space to fit a hazelnut after each bulb.

Fill the gaps between the bulbs of cream with hazelnuts.

Sandwich with the other half of the bun. Dust with icing/confectioners' sugar, to serve.

VARIATION

Christmas: stir 1–2 tablespoons brandy into the crème pâtissière. Blitz some icing/confectioners' sugar with any leftover hazelnuts to create a hazelnut sugar. Add ground spices of your choice, such as cinnamon, mixed spice/apple pie spice, nutmeg, ginger etc.

Chocolate and coffee éclairs

Certain things are loved all over the world. Coffee, chocolate and éclairs are three of them, so I decided to combine these to create an amazing taste sensation that will instantly arouse your taste buds. The classic éclair is part of the foundations of French culinary history. It is likely to have been invented in the nineteenth century by Antoine Carême, one of the most celebrated original French pastry chefs, billed as the first celebrity chef and the craftsman behind Napoleon's wedding cake. Chef, enjoy!

Eclairs

1 x quantity Pâte à Choux (page 18)
1 x quantity Crème Pâtissière (page 25), chilled
50–100 g/1½–3½ oz. dark chocolate (Cuban origin, 70% cocoa, if you can find it), chopped
150 g/1 cup cocoa nibs (available online)

Coffee ganache

100 ml/½ cup double/heavy cream
2 teaspoons instant coffee granules
1 teaspoon coffee liqueur
50 g/1½ oz. dark chocolate (Cuban origin, 70% cocoa), chopped
2 teaspoons butter

baking sheet, lined with greaseproof paper
piping bag fitted with a plain nozzle/tip

Makes about 10

For the éclairs
Preheat the oven to 180°C (350°F) Gas 4.

Make the Pâte à Choux following the instructions on page 18 and pipe into oval éclairs about 10 cm/4 inches long on the prepared baking sheet.

Bake in the preheated oven for 10–15 minutes or until puffed up and golden, then turn the oven off and leave the éclairs inside to cool completely and dry out.

Melt the chocolate on low power in a microwave or in a heatproof bowl over a pan of simmering water (not letting the base of the bowl touch the water).

Make the Crème Pâtissière following the instructions on page 25, then fold in the melted chocolate at the end. Allow to cool completely before using.

For the coffee ganache
Put the cream, coffee granules and liqueur in a saucepan and bring to the boil over low heat.

Pour the boiled cream into a wide, heatproof bowl and add the chocolate and butter. Using a spatula, start to mix the ingredients in a circular motion, just in the centre of the bowl. Keep mixing in a tight circle until the chocolate starts to melt and emulsify with the liquid. Gradually widen the circle until all the chocolate has melted and you have a shiny, smooth ganache.

Take a cooled éclair and dip the top into the ganache. Shake off any excess, turn up the right way round and allow to cool and set slightly on a wire rack. Repeat with the remaining éclairs.

Give each éclair a second dip in the ganache and allow to set again.

Give each éclair a third and final dip in the ganache to make a thick, dense topping. Allow to set completely.

When the ganache has set, carefully cut each éclair in half horizontally.

Fill the piping bag with chocolate crème pâtissière and pipe a generous coil along the cut side of the bottom half of each éclair.

Sandwich with the other half of the éclair. Sprinkle cocoa nibs over the top of the éclairs for a crunchy finish.

Mango and passionfruit mini éclairs

These little éclairs are divine – for afternoon tea or part of an 'assiette' of desserts or even as sweet canapés! Filled with a punchy tropical pastry cream and topped with a crunchy crumble, these beauties will definitely have your guests asking for more!

Crumble topping

80 g/5 tablespoons butter, softened

100 g/½ cup light brown sugar

100 g/¾ cup plain/all-purpose flour

Eclairs

1 x quantity Pâte à Choux (page 18)

1 quantity Crème Diplomate (page 26, made with mango and passionfruit Crème Pâtissière)

baking sheets, lined with greaseproof paper

piping bag fitted with a plain nozzle/tip

Makes about 20

For the crumble topping

Beat the butter and sugar together in a stand mixer or in a bowl with an electric whisk just until well combined.

Add the flour and bring together into a dough with your hands. Turn the dough out onto a sheet of greaseproof paper, top with another sheet and flatten with a rolling pin until about 3 mm/⅛ inch thick. Freeze for 1 hour.

For the éclairs

Preheat the oven to 180°C (350°F) Gas 4.

Make the Pâte à Choux following the instructions on page 18 and pipe into ovals about 5 cm/2 inches on the prepared baking sheets. These will be mini éclairs.

Take the crumble topping out of the freezer, remove the top sheet of paper and cut into long, slim rectangles to fit on the éclairs. Cut out the same number as there are éclairs and place a rectangle on top of each éclair.

Bake in the preheated oven for 10–12 minutes or until puffed up and golden, then turn the oven off and leave the éclairs inside to cool completely and dry out.

Carefully cut each cooled éclair in half horizontally. Fill the piping bag with Crème Diplomate and pipe a generous coil along the cut side of the bottom half of each éclair.

Sandwich with the other half of the éclair.

If you like, in order to boost the mango flavour in this recipe, you could put some mango flesh and icing/confectioners' sugar in a blender and process until smooth. Spoon some of this on the bottom half of each éclair, then pipe the Crème Diplomate over it.

Spiced rum babas

Originally from the Alsace region of France, this little yeast cake drenched in rum syrup was originally made using Kugelhopf, a German leavened cake dough. Raisins and other dried fruits were added to a lighter version and that became the rum baba. One of the best rum babas I have ever eaten was at The Waterside Inn, by Alain Roux: just delicious, plain and simple, lovely syrup and some chantilly cream – it's all you need.

75 ml/⅓ cup milk
10 g/⅔ cake fresh yeast or 5 g/2 teaspoons dried yeast
4 teaspoons sugar
150 g/1 cup plus 2 tablespoons strong white bread flour
a pinch of salt
2 eggs
75 g/5 tablespoons butter, melted

Syrup
1 orange
1 lemon
400 ml/1⅔ cups water
400 g/2 cups sugar
1 cinnamon stick
2 star anise
1 vanilla bean, split
150 ml/⅔ cup dark rum

piping bag fitted with a plain nozzle/tip (optional)
6 silicone dariole moulds or 6-hole silicone muffin pan

Makes 6

Warm the milk in saucepan until hand hot. Transfer to a bowl with the yeast and stir until the yeast has dissolved.

Either in a mixing bowl with a wooden spoon, or in a stand mixer with a dough hook, mix the sugar, flour and salt together, then pour in the yeast mixture and eggs. Mix slowly until the mixture comes together into a dough. Mix well with your hands or the dough hook until the dough is smooth and elastic. **(A)**

Gradually beat in the butter. **(B)**

Pipe or spoon the dough into the dariole moulds or muffin pan. **(C)**

Allow to rise in a warm place or near a hot oven for 10–15 minutes. **(D)**

Preheat the oven to 200°C (400°F) Gas 6.

Bake the rum babas in the preheated oven for 20 minutes or until golden and risen.

For the syrup
Cut the peel off the orange and lemon (avoiding the bitter white pith underneath) in large chunks. Put in a large saucepan with the remaining ingredients and bring to the boil. Once boiled, turn the heat down to its lowest setting and allow the syrup to become just warm.

Put the rum babas in the syrup and let them soak up some of it and expand slightly.

Serve with some of the syrup on the side.

Classic millefeuille

Look in any French pâtisserie window and you're likely to see a millefeuille of some description. Made in individual portions, as below, or as a large cake, the simplest version is filled with crème pâtissière and finished with a dusting of icing/confectioners' sugar or a thin layer of fondant glaze. If you bake the puff pastry between two baking sheets, it will stop it puffing up too much and instead render an ultra crisp base that will crack oh-so-satisfyingly when you push your dessert fork through it. Classy, delicious and pure joy to eat!

250 g/9 oz. Pâte Feuilletée (page 16), or storebought puff pastry
icing/confectioners' sugar, to dust
1 x quantity Crème Pâtissière (page 25)

baking sheet, lined with greaseproof paper
piping bag fitted with a plain nozzle/tip

Makes 6–8

Preheat the oven to 190°C (375°F) Gas 5.

Using a rolling pin, roll out the pastry on a lightly floured surface until 5 mm/¼ inch thick.

Transfer the pastry to the prepared baking sheet. Dust it with icing/confectioners' sugar. Lay a piece of greaseproof paper over the top, then place another baking sheet over that. This will stop the pastry from rising too much and will also help to caramelize it.

Bake in the preheated oven for 10 minutes, then take the top baking sheet and piece of greaseproof paper off the top and return the pastry to the oven to bake for a further 10 minutes or until golden brown and crispy. Allow to cool completely.

Very gently lay the sheet of baked puff pastry on a chopping/cutting board. Using a serrated knife, carefully cut the pastry into neat rectangles, about 10 x 5 cm/4 x 2 inches. You will need 3 rectangles for each millefeuille. Set the 6–8 best-looking rectangles aside for the top layer of the millefeuilles and dust icing/confectioners' sugar liberally over them.

Fill a piping bag with Crème Pâtissière. Pipe 2 rows of 4 bulbs on all the pastry rectangles (except the reserved top ones).

Build up the millefeuilles by laying one piped rectangle on top of another. Top with a reserved, sugar-dusted rectangle.

Raspberry and rose millefeuilles

The millefeuille is a French institution. Meaning 'a thousand leaves', it consists of wonderful layers of crisp puff pastry. When I did my chef's training, I made an apple millefeuille dessert – layer upon layer of caramelized apples, served with apple sorbet. It was for a dinner that my grandad came to, and I remember him telling me afterwards that it I shouldn't have called it a millefeuille because it was not pastry. Sorry Grandad! This recipe is my little twist on the French classic, perfect for a summer's day, with fresh raspberries, delicate rose flavours and served with a glass of rosé Champagne.

250 g/9 oz. Pâte Feuilletée (page 16), or storebought puff pastry
½ quantity Crème Diplomate (page 26)
1 teaspoon rose water
1 punnet raspberries
icing/confectioners' sugar, to dust

6-cm/2½-inch cookie cutter
baking sheet, lined with greaseproof paper
piping bag fitted with a plain nozzle/tip
kitchen blowtorch

Makes about 8

Preheat the oven to 180°C (350°F) Gas 4.

Using a rolling pin, roll out the pastry on a lightly floured surface until 5 mm/¼ inch thick.

Stamp out about 8 rounds using the cookie cutter and arrange them on the prepared baking sheet.

Bake the rounds of pastry in the preheated oven for about 10 minutes or until puffed up and golden. Allow to cool completely.

Make the Crème Diplomate following the instructions on page 26, then fold in the rose water at the end.

Using a serrated knife, cut through each pastry round twice, horizontally, to make 3 layers.

Fill the piping bag with crème diplomate and pipe 4 bulbs of cream around the rim of the flat layers of pastry (leave the domed layers for the tops of the millefeuilles). Leave space to fit a raspberry after each bulb.

Pipe a bulb in the centre of each pastry round.

Fill the gaps between the bulbs of cream with upside-down raspberries.

Lay all the pastry tops, domed side up, on a heatproof surface and dust them liberally with icing/confectioners' sugar. Briefly blast them with a kitchen blowtorch to caramelize them and give them extra crunch.

Petits savarins with berries and cream

A variation on the rum baba, a savarin can be made large or small using the same dough, which is baked in a ring-shaped mould. It is named after the celebrated lawyer and gastronome Brillat-Savarin, who also has a cheese named after him. I like to saturate my savarins in Grand Marnier which gives them a lovely orange flavour. Simply filled with chantilly and some seasonal berries, it's a delightfully refined dessert.

75 ml/⅓ cup milk
10 g/⅔ cake fresh yeast or 5 g/2 teaspoons dried yeast
4 teaspoons sugar
150 g/1 cup plus 2 tablespoons strong white bread flour
a pinch of salt
2 eggs
75 g/5 tablespoons butter, melted
½ quantity Crème Chantilly (page 26)
fresh berries of your choice, to serve

Syrup
1 orange
1 lemon
500 ml/2 cups water
400 g/2 cups sugar
1 vanilla bean, split
dash of Grand Marnier

piping bag fitted with a plain nozzle/tip (optional)
2 x 6-hole mini savarin or ring doughnut pans

Makes 12

Warm the milk in saucepan until hand hot. Transfer to a bowl with the yeast and stir until the yeast has dissolved.

Either in a mixing bowl with a wooden spoon, or in a stand mixer with a dough hook, mix the sugar, flour and salt together, then pour in the yeast mixture and eggs. Mix slowly until the mixture comes together into a dough. Mix well with your hands or the dough hook until the dough is smooth and elastic.

Gradually beat in the butter.

Pipe or spoon the dough into the savarin or ring doughnut pans.

Allow to rise in a warm place or near a hot oven for 10–15 minutes.

Preheat the oven to 200°C (400°F) Gas 6.

Bake the savarins in the preheated oven for 20 minutes or until golden and risen.

For the syrup

Cut the peel off the orange and lemon (avoiding the bitter white pith) in large chunks. Put in a large saucepan with the remaining ingredients and bring to the boil. Once boiled, turn the heat down to its lowest setting and allow the syrup to become just warm.

Put the savarins in the syrup and let them soak up some of it and expand slightly.

Allow the savarins to cool completely, then fill the holes with a spoonful of Crème Chantilly and top with fresh berries of your choice.

To bump up the flavour, you can brush hot marmalade over the soaked savarins.

SPECIALITE
DE
TARTES CHAUDES
SALEES
A TOUTE HEURE
POM'CANNELL
RESTAURAN
SALON DE TH
PATISSERIES
GLACES

Tarts are so often a means by which to showcase the best seasonal fruit that you can buy. Start with a basic pastry dough and use it to line one of so many types of tart pan available these days – plain, fluted, shallow, deep, large, medium or small – then fill it with divine vanilla-specked crème pâtissière and a tantalizing layer of strawberries, picked at the height of summer when they are at their reddest and ripest. There really is no more satisfying dessert than this at the close of a sun-drenched lunch. But of course the possibilities and variations are endless, from the richest of dark chocolate tarts, to the tangiest of lemon ones.

Tarts

Tarte au chocolat

As a self-confessed chocolate lover, I don't think it gets better than a really good chocolate tart. When I was training, I remember trying to make some really difficult recipes by amazing French pastry chefs that I could never make work. Then I learnt how to make chocolate ganache, which is the basis of my chocolate tart. Traditionally a chocolate tart is baked, but by using a ganache, you can make it the night before, leave it out of the fridge and you are left with a beautiful, smooth, rich and indulgent tart that is very easy to eat – and most likely finish off too. I've used a mixture of milk and dark chocolate to deliver a balanced, not-too-bitter flavour.

1 x quantity Pâte Sablée (page 12, but replace one-third of the flour with cocoa powder)
25 g/1 oz. dark chocolate
Chocolate Curls (page 33), to decorate

Filling
150 ml/⅔ cup whipping cream
2 tablespoons butter
a pinch of salt
100 g/3½ oz. milk chocolate, chopped
175 g/6 oz. dark chocolate, chopped

20-cm/8-in. tart pan, greased and lightly dusted with flour
baking beans

Serves 6–8

Preheat the oven to 180°C (350°F) Gas 4.

Take the Pâte Sablée out of the fridge and put on a lightly floured surface. Using a rolling pin, roll it out to a rough circle at about 25 cm/10 inches in diameter.

Loosely wrap the dough around the rolling pin and transfer it to the prepared tart pan. Unravel the dough into the pan. Gently coax the dough neatly into the curves and angles of the pan, press lightly into the sides and cut off any excess with a small, sharp knife.

Lay a sheet of greaseproof paper over the pan and fill it with baking beans. Put the pan on a baking sheet and bake in the preheated oven for about 10–15 minutes.

Lower the oven temperature to 160°C (325°F) Gas 3. Remove the paper and beans from the tart pan and return the tart case to the oven for 5–10 minutes.

Remove the tart case from the oven and allow to cool completely, then remove from the pan.

Meanwhile, melt the chocolate on low power in a microwave or in a heatproof bowl over a pan of simmering water (not letting the base of the bowl touch the water).

Brush the melted chocolate inside the cooled tart case. This will not only prevent the pastry from going soggy when the filling is added, but it will also provide another chocolate hit.

For the filling

Put the cream, butter and salt in a saucepan and bring to the boil over low heat.

Pour the boiled cream into a heatproof bowl and add the chocolates. Using a spatula, start to mix the ingredients in a circular motion, just in the centre of the bowl. Keep mixing in a tight circle until the chocolate starts to melt and emulsify with the liquid. Gradually widen the circle until all the chocolate has melted and you have a shiny, smooth ganache.

Pour the filling straight into the tart case and allow to set overnight at room temperature.

To serve, scatter chocolate curls all over the tart. Cut a slice and see how long the rest survives for!

A

B

Salted caramel and chocolate tartlets

If one flavour has dominated the food world over the last few years, it has to be salted caramel. You see it everywhere, from high-street supermarkets, to upmarket pâtisseries and even fast-food restaurants. You can add salted nuts to the caramel to give you a Snickers feel, but I like to caramelize mine and scatter them on top of the tartlets with elegant shards of chocolate.

1 x quantity Pâte Sablée (page 12)
25 g/1 oz. dark chocolate
½ quantity Crème Diplomate (page 26)
Caramelized Nuts and Chocolate Shards (page 33)

Salted caramel
125 g/⅔ cup sugar
75 ml/⅓ cup whipping cream
1 vanilla bean
1½ tablespoons butter
½ teaspoon salt

Filling
150 ml/⅔ cup whipping cream
2 tablespoons butter
a pinch of salt
275 g/10 oz. dark chocolate, chopped

6 individual tartlet pans, greased and dusted with flour
baking beans

Makes 6

Preheat the oven to 180°C (350°F) Gas 4.

Take the Pâte Sablée out of the fridge and divide it into 6 equal portions. Using a rolling pin, roll out each portion on a lightly floured surface to a rough circle slightly larger than the diameter of the tartlet pans.

Loosely wrap one portion of dough at a time around the rolling pin and transfer it to a prepared tartlet pan. Unravel the dough into the pan. Gently coax the dough neatly into the curves and angles of the pan, press lightly into the sides and cut off any excess with a small, sharp knife.

Lay a piece of greaseproof paper over each pan and fill it with baking beans. Put all the pans on a baking sheet and bake in the preheated oven for about 10–15 minutes.

Lower the oven temperature to 160°C (325°F) Gas 3. Remove the paper and beans from the tartlet pans and return the tartlet cases to the oven for 5 minutes.

Remove the tartlet cases from the oven and allow to cool completely, then remove from the pans.

Meanwhile, melt the chocolate on low power in a microwave or in a heatproof bowl over a pan of simmering water (not letting the base of the bowl touch the water).

Brush the melted chocolate inside the cooled tartlet cases. **(A)**

C

D

E

F

For the salted caramel

Put the sugar in a saucepan over low heat. Leave it to heat and melt without being tempted to stir it.

Meanwhile, in a separate saucepan, bring the cream to the boil over low heat.

The sugar will begin to caramelize around the edges. Don't stir it, even now, otherwise the sugar will crystallize irreparably. When all the sugar has turned deep but not dark golden, stir it with a silicone spatula, breaking down any little bits of sugar. You now have caramel – a loose golden syrup ready for the volcanic bit coming up.

Over low heat, slowly and very carefully pour in the boiled cream, in stages. The cream and caramel will combust and bubble up, but don't be scared – this is good. Once the cream has been stirred in, pour in another batch and continue until all the cream has been used up. **(B)**

Split the vanilla bean lengthwise using a small, sharp knife and scrape the seeds out into the pan. Keep stirring over low heat for a minute or so, then add the butter and salt. Remove from the heat and stir until the butter has melted.

Allow the caramel to cool for 10 minutes, then divide equally between the tartlet cases. It should reach just under halfway up the cases. **(C)**

Allow to set while you make the filling.

For the filling

Put the cream, butter and salt in a saucepan and bring to the boil over low heat.

Pour the boiled cream into a heatproof bowl and add the chocolate. Using a spatula, start to mix the ingredients in a circular motion, just in the centre of the bowl. Keep mixing in a tight circle until the chocolate starts to melt and emulsify with the liquid. Gradually widen the circle until all the chocolate has melted and you have a shiny, smooth ganache.

Spoon the filling evenly over the caramel layer in the tartlet cases. **(D)**

Allow to set overnight at room temperature.

The next day, to serve, make quenelles for decoration. Put the Crème Diplomate in a bowl and take a tablespoon. Drag the tablespoon through the cream, skimming just below the surface. When the spoon reaches the edge of the bowl, drag it up the edge of the bowl to smooth the cream inside the spoon. You should get an egg-shaped portion of cream. Place it top of a tartlet and repeat the process to make 5 more quenelles for the remaining tartlets. **(E)**

Make the Caramelized Nuts and Chocolate Shards following the instructions on page 33. **(F)**

To serve, stick some chocolate shards into each tartlet and garnish with caramelized nuts.

Tarte au citron

I couldn't write a book on French pastry without including a recipe for lemon tart. It is so famous in France, but also commonly found on many restaurant dessert menus in London. This recipe was given to me by a great friend of mine, Martin Caws. He was head chef at the Michelin-starred Mirabelle in Mayfair, and he has worked with chefs such as Tom Aikens and Raymond Blanc. This lemon tart was always on his menu and it sold out every night!

1 x quantity Pâte Sucrée (page 12)
icing/confectioners' sugar, to dust

Filling
9 eggs
390 g/2 cups sugar
juice and grated zest of 5 lemons
275 ml/1 cup plus 2 tablespoons double/heavy cream

20-cm/8-in. tart pan, greased and lightly dusted with flour
baking beans

Serves 6–8

Preheat the oven to 180°C (350°F) Gas 4.

Take the Pâte Sucrée out of the fridge and put on a lightly floured surface. Using a rolling pin, roll it out to a rough circle at about 25 cm/10 inches in diameter.

Loosely wrap the dough around the rolling pin and transfer it to the prepared tart pan. Unravel the dough into the pan. Gently coax the dough neatly into the curves and angles of the pan, press lightly into the sides and cut off any excess with a small, sharp knife.

Lay a sheet of greaseproof paper over the pan and fill it with baking beans. Put the pan on a baking sheet and bake in the preheated oven for about 10–15 minutes.

Lower the oven temperature to 160°C (325°F) Gas 3. Remove the paper and beans from the tart pan and return the tart case to the oven for 5–10 minutes. Remove from the oven.

Lower the oven temperature to 130°C (250°F) Gas ½.

For the filling

Put the eggs and sugar in a mixing bowl and whisk with a balloon whisk just to combine. Whisk in the lemon juice and zest.

Finally, stir in the cream. Pour the mixture into a jug/pitcher.

Put the blind-baked tart case back into the oven, as far forward as you can without the pan falling off the oven shelf. Pour the filling slowly and carefully into the tart case.

Push the tart further into the oven, close the door, say a little prayer and bake for about 30–40 minutes or until it just starts to set in the centre but still wobbles like a jelly. It will continue to cook when it is taken out of the oven, so don't be tempted to keep baking until it is fully set because it will curdle and split.

Allow to cool completely, then remove from the pan.

To serve, dust the tart with icing/confectioners' sugar and serve at room temperature.

Lemon and yuzu meringue tart

I wanted to update the classic tarte au citron with an unusual flavour and an old-fashioned technique. Yuzu is a Japanese citrus fruit, like a hybrid of lemon and lime with a hint of mandarin. I like to top my lemon tart with meringue, piped high and flambéed at the dinner table with a blowtorch!

1 x quantity Pâte Sablée (page 12)
25 g/1 oz. white chocolate

Lemon and yuzu curd
2 tablespoons yuzu juice (available online or in good Japanese supermarkets)
juice and grated zest of 2 lemons
3 egg yolks
100 g/½ cup raw cane sugar
2 tablespoons butter, chilled and diced

Meringue topping
100 g/½ cup sugar
2 tablespoons water
3 egg whites

20-cm/8-in. fluted tart pan, greased and lightly dusted with flour
baking beans
sugar thermometer
piping bag fitted with a plain nozzle/tip
kitchen blowtorch (optional)

Serves 6–8

Preheat the oven to 180°C (350°F) Gas 4.

Take the Pâte Sablée out of the fridge and put on a lightly floured surface. Using a rolling pin, roll it out to a rough circle at about 25 cm/10 inches in diameter.

Loosely wrap the dough around the rolling pin and transfer it to the prepared tart pan. Unravel the dough into the pan. Gently coax the dough neatly into the curves and angles of the pan, press lightly into the sides and cut off any excess with a small, sharp knife.

Lay a sheet of greaseproof paper over the pan and fill it with baking beans. Put the pan on a baking sheet and bake in the preheated oven for about 10–15 minutes.

Lower the oven temperature to 160°C (325°F) Gas 3. Remove the paper and beans from the tart pan and return the tart case to the oven for 5–10 minutes. Remove the tart case from the oven and allow to cool completely, then remove from the pan.

Meanwhile, melt the chocolate on low power in a microwave or in a heatproof bowl over a pan of simmering water (not letting the base of the bowl touch the water). Brush the melted chocolate inside the cooled tart case.

For the lemon and yuzu curd

Put the yuzu juice, juice of 1 lemon and all the lemon zest in a saucepan and bring to the boil over low heat.

Put the egg yolks and sugar in a mixing bowl and whisk with a balloon whisk until it looks like the sugar has dissolved. Very slowly pour the boiled citrus juice into the mixing bowl, whisking constantly. Pour the mixture back into the pan, set over medium heat and stir. It will start to thicken and resemble thick, glossy curd.

Now remove it from the heat and whisk in the butter, one piece at a time. Mix until all the butter has melted. Finally, pour the curd into the tart case and allow to cool completely.

For the meringue

Put the sugar and water in a saucepan and bring to the boil. Simmer over low heat until the syrup reaches 121°C/250°F on a sugar thermometer.

Meanwhile, put the egg whites and remaining lemon juice in a stand mixer and begin whisking. until stiff peaks form. Once the syrup has reached the right temperature, slowly pour it in a steady stream into the meringue bowl with the beaters still running. Avoid letting the syrup touch the beaters. Keep whisking until you have used up all the syrup and the meringue is glossy, thick and has cooled substantially – this may take several minutes of whisking. The bowl itself must have cooled too.

Fill the piping bag with meringue and pipe bulbs of different sizes onto the curd in the tart case.

To serve, blast the meringue with a kitchen blowtorch or under a very hot grill/broiler.

Tarte aux pommes

French apple tart cannot be beaten outside of France; they make it so well, whether rustic or immaculate. It usually consists of a sweet shortcrust pastry filled with apple compote and neatly fanned and glazed apple slices on top, I prefer to fill mine with homemade apple jam, frangipane and lots of chunky apples glazed with more of the apple jam.

1 x quantity Pâte Sucrée (page 12)
1 x quantity Frangipane (page 29)
grated zest of 2 lemons
flaked/slivered almonds, to decorate (optional)
4 Granny Smith apples, peeled, cored and sliced into wedges
50 g/¼ cup apricot jam
1 tablespoon water

Apple jam
600 g/1¼ lbs. Bramley or other tart apples, peeled, cored and roughly chopped
100 ml/⅓ cup water
juice and grated zest of 2 lemons
250 g/1¼ cups fruit sugar

20-cm/8-in. fluted tart pan, greased and lightly dusted with flour

Serves 6–8

Take the Pâte Sucrée out of the fridge and put on a lightly floured surface. Using a rolling pin, roll it out to a rough circle at about 25 cm/10 inches in diameter.

Loosely wrap the dough around the rolling pin and transfer it to the prepared tart pan. Unravel the dough into the pan. Gently coax the dough neatly into the curves and angles of the pan, press lightly into the sides and cut off any excess with a small, sharp knife.

Put the tart pan on a baking sheet and refrigerate while you make the apple jam.

For the apple jam

Put the apples, water, lemon juice and zest in a large saucepan over low heat and cook for about 20 minutes, or until the apples have broken down and are soft and fluffy in texture.

Add the fruit sugar, turn up the heat and cook for 5–10 minutes until the sugar has dissolved and the mixture has become thick and jam-like.

Remove from the heat and allow to cool completely before using.

Preheat the oven to 180°C (350°F) Gas 4.

Remove the tart case from the fridge. Spoon in enough apple jam to coat the base of the case and spread it evenly. Reserve the remaining jam.

Make the Frangipane following the instructions on page 29 and stir in the lemon zest at the end.

Spoon the frangipane on top of the jam and spread it evenly.

Arrange the wedges of apple haphazardly or elegantly (whichever you prefer!) over the frangipane. Place the flaked/slivered almonds, if using, around the edge of the tart.

Bake in the preheated oven for 30–45 minutes depending on the thickness of the tart. Test if the tart is done by inserting a skewer in the middle (try not to go all the way through in case you damage the pastry on the bottom) – if it comes out clean, it is ready.

Meanwhile, to make a glaze, put 50 g/¼ cup of the reserved apple jam, the apricot jam and water in a small saucepan and bring to the boil.

When the tart comes out of the oven, brush the glaze immediately over the top. When the tart cools, the glaze will set to a beautiful shine.

Allow to cool slightly before removing the tart from the pan. Serve with Crème Chantilly (page 26) or crème fraîche to cut through the richness.

Any leftover apple jam can be made into lovely gifts – add ground cinnamon to taste, then transfer to sterilized jars.

Pear and chocolate tartlets

The much-loved French dessert, Poires Belle-Hélène, was invented in the nineteenth century by the great chef Auguste Escoffier. Featuring poached pears, vanilla ice cream, rich chocolate sauce and often also almonds, it inspired me to create this tart. I made something very similar during my training and served it with mulled-wine ice cream. Delicious!

Poached pears

4 Conference pears (or canned pears, in which case you don't need to poach them)
200 g/1 cup sugar
juice and grated zest of 3 lemons
1 vanilla bean, split
3 tablespoons Poire William liqueur
750 ml (1 bottle) white wine

Tartlet cases

1 x quantity Pâte Sucrée (page 12)
1 x quantity Chocolate and Hazelnut Frangipane (page 29)
3 tablespoons flaked/slivered almonds
50 g/¼ cup apricot jam
1 tablespoon water

6–8 individual tartlet pans, greased and lightly dusted with flour

Makes 6–8

For the poached pears

Peel and core the pears and put them a medium saucepan with the sugar, lemon juice and zest, vanilla bean, Poire William and white wine. Bring to the boil.

Cut a disc of greaseproof paper to fit snugly inside the saucepan. Lay it on top of the poaching liquid, lower the heat and gently poach the pears for 20–30 minutes. The pears should not get too soft as they will be cooked further when they are in the tartlets.

Remove the pan from the heat, fish the pears out with a slotted spoon and allow to cool on a plate. I would encourage you to keep the cooking liquor and make a granita or sorbet with it later – it will be full of flavour.

For the tartlet cases

Preheat the oven to 180°C (350°F) Gas 4.

Take the Pâte Sucrée out of the fridge and divide it into 6–8 equal portions. Using a rolling pin, roll out each portion on a lightly floured surface to a rough circle slightly larger than the diameter of the tartlet pans.

Loosely wrap one portion of dough at a time around the rolling pin and transfer to a prepared tartlet pan. Unravel the dough into the pan. Gently coax the dough neatly into the curves and angles of the pan, press lightly into the sides and cut off any excess with a small, sharp knife.

Put the tartlet pans on a baking sheet and refrigerate for 1 hour.

Remove the tartlet cases from the fridge.

Divide the Chocolate and Hazelnut Frangipane equally between the tartlet cases and spread level with a spatula.

Cut the cooled, poached pears into large chunks so that they fit inside the tartlet cases. Arrange them in the cases, then sprinkle the almonds over the top.

Bake the tartlets in the preheated oven for 30 minutes depending on the thickness of the tartlets. Test if they are done by inserting a skewer in the middle (try not to go all the way through in case you damage the pastry on the bottom) – if it comes out clean, they are ready.

Meanwhile, to make a glaze, put the apricot jam and water in a small saucepan and bring to the boil. If the glaze looks too thick, you can add a little poaching liquor or Poire William.

When the tartlets come out of the oven, brush the glaze immediately over the tops. When they cool, the glaze will set to a beautiful shine.

Allow to cool slightly before removing the tartlets from the pans. They must, of course, be served with vanilla ice cream and rich, dark chocolate sauce – a salute to Escoffier!

Tarte aux fraises

Strawberry tart is such a time-honoured dessert and was one of the first pastries I learnt how to make. Served in pâtisseries, restaurants, tea rooms, cafés and homes, especially for afternoon tea, this surely is a favourite on both sides of the Channel. Somehow, strawberries, vanilla cream and crumbly pastry scream of summer, so this is one to make with perfectly ripe strawberries when the sun is shining.

1 x quantity Pâte Sablée (page 12)
1 x quantity Crème Pâtissière (page 25)
250 g/9 oz. strawberries
50 g/¼ cup apricot jam
1 tablespoon water

20-cm/8-in. fluted tart pan, greased and lightly dusted with flour
baking beans

Serves 6–8

Preheat the oven to 180°C (350°F) Gas 4.

Take the Pâte Sablée out of the fridge and put on a lightly floured surface. Using a rolling pin, roll it out to a rough circle at about 25 cm/10 inches in diameter.

Loosely wrap the dough around the rolling pin and transfer it to the prepared tart pan. Unravel the dough into the pan. Gently coax the dough neatly into the curves and angles of the pan, press lightly into the sides and cut off any excess with a small, sharp knife.

Lay a sheet of greaseproof paper over the pan and fill it with baking beans. Put the pan on a baking sheet and bake in the preheated oven for about 10–15 minutes.

Lower the oven temperature to 160°C (325°F) Gas 3. Remove the paper and beans from the tart pan and return the tart case to the oven for 5–10 minutes.

Remove the tart case from the oven and allow to cool completely, then remove from the pan.

Spoon the Crème Pâtissière into the tart case and spread level with a spatula.

Cut the stalks off the strawberries in a straight line across the tops. At the same time, try to get all the strawberries roughly the same height; this will make them particularly impressive when you arrange them on the tart. Now slice the strawberries quite thinly.

Arrange them, in concentric circles on the crème pâtissière, starting from the outer edge and working towards the middle, and placing every strawberry in the same direction.

To make a glaze, put the apricot jam and water in a small saucepan and bring to the boil. Brush it gently all over the strawberries.

VARIATIONS

The key with this tart is to keep it simple. Let the fruit be the hero and celebrate it with the best in-season produce you can buy.

Scottish-style: replace the strawberries with raspberries, add a dash of whisky to the Crème Pâtissière and scatter caramelized oats on top (see page 33 and follow the instructions for caramelizing nuts).

Tropical: replace the strawberries with sliced mango or papaya and scatter passionfruit over the top.

Strawberry and pistachio tartlets

I like to make well-known recipes my own, so to give a modern twist to the beloved strawberry tart, I suggest adding pistachio paste to the crème pâtissière filling. It gives an amazing vibrant green colour and flavour that works so well with juicy strawberries. Pistachio paste can be bought online, or to make your own – it's dead easy – follow my instructions below.

1 x quantity Pâte Sablée (page 12)
50 g/¼ cup pistachio paste (storebought, or to make your own, see method here)
1 x quantity Crème Pâtissière (page 25, adding the pistachio paste to the milk)
25 g/1 oz. white chocolate
250 g/9 oz. strawberries
50 g/⅓ cup pistachios, finely chopped

6 individual tartlet pans, greased and lightly dusted with flour
baking beans

Makes 6

Preheat the oven to 180°C (350°F) Gas 4.

Take the Pâte Sablée out of the fridge and divide it into 6 equal portions. Using a rolling pin, roll out each portion on a lightly floured surface to a rough circle slightly larger than the diameter of the tartlet pans.

Loosely wrap one portion of dough at a time around the rolling pin and transfer it to a prepared tartlet pan. Unravel the dough into the pan. Gently coax the dough neatly into the curves and angles of the pan, press lightly into the sides and cut off any excess with a small, sharp knife.

Lay a piece of greaseproof paper over each pan and fill it with baking beans. Put all the pans on a baking sheet and bake in the preheated oven for about 10–15 minutes.

Lower the oven temperature to 160°C (325°F) Gas 3. Remove the paper and beans from the tartlet pans and return the tartlet cases to the oven for 5 minutes.

Remove the tartlet cases from the oven and allow to cool completely, then remove from the pans.

Meanwhile, melt the chocolate on low power in a microwave or in a heatproof bowl over a pan of simmering water (not letting the base of the bowl touch the water).

Brush the melted chocolate inside the cooled tartlet cases.

Divide the pistachio Crème Pâtissière evenly between the tartlet cases.

Hull the strawberries and cut them in halves or quarters, depending on their size.

Top the tartlets with the strawberries and chopped pistachios.

PISTACHIO PASTE

To make your own pistachio paste, put 100 g/⅔ cup pistachios and 50 g/¼ cup sugar into a heavy-based saucepan and continually stir over medium heat until the sugar crystallizes around the nuts and they turn golden. Remove from the heat and scatter onto a sheet of greaseproof paper. Allow to cool completely. Break the cooled nuts into pieces and put in a food processor. Process to a powder, then add 1 tablespoon vegetable oil and process again until you get a paste. Store, refrigerated, in an airtight container for up to 2 weeks.

Tarte éxotique

This is your chance to serve up a real showpiece! Go all out with the tropical fruit, which nestle on an unexpected base of tropical crème patissière, bursting with flavour. This tart reminds me of my first trip to Paris when I was amazed by the jewelled fruits piled high on tartlets in pâtisserie windows. I hope yours looks as good as one of them!

1 x quantity Pâte Sablée (page 12)
1 x quantity mango and passionfruit Crème Pâtissière (page 25)
3 tablespoons Malibu rum
tropical or colourful fruits of your choice, eg mango, kiwi, papaya, figs, starfruit, physalis, passionfruit, pineapple, cut into chunks if large

20-cm/8-in. fluted tart pan, greased and lightly dusted with flour
baking beans

Serves 6–8

Preheat the oven to 180°C (350°F) Gas 4.

Take the Pâte Sablée out of the fridge and put on a lightly floured surface. Using a rolling pin, roll it out to a rough circle at about 25 cm/10 inches in diameter.

Loosely wrap the dough around the rolling pin and transfer it to the prepared tart pan. Unravel the dough into the pan. Gently coax the dough neatly into the curves and angles of the pan, press lightly into the sides and cut off any excess with a small, sharp knife.

Lay a sheet of greaseproof paper over the pan and fill it with baking beans. Put the pan on a baking sheet and bake in the preheated oven for about 10–15 minutes.

Lower the oven temperature to 160°C (325°F) Gas 3. Remove the paper and beans from the tart pan and return the tart case to the oven for 5–10 minutes.

Remove the tart case from the oven and allow to cool completely, then remove from the pan.

Make the Crème Pâtissière following the instructions on page 25 and stir the Malibu rum in at the end.

Spoon the cream into the tart case and spread level with a spatula. Pile the fruit up in the tart case, any way you like!

Tarte croustillante aux abricots

There are as many varieties of apricot tart in France as there are of the ubiquitous apple tart. In Normandy, for example, they bake the apricots with custard. I wanted more lightness and crunch so I use apricot compote, apricot crème diplomate, fresh apricot wedges and a sprinkling of crumble!

1 x quantity Pâte à Sablé Breton (page 15)
1 x quantity Crème Diplomate (page 26, made with apricot Crème Pâtissiere)
icing/confectioners' sugar, to dust

Apricot crumble
150 g/1 cup semi-dried apricots
70 g/5 tablespoons butter
100 g/¾ cup plain/all-purpose flour
100 g/1 cup ground almonds
grated zest of 1 lemon

Apricot compote
200 g/7 oz. apricots
2 teaspoons butter
50 g/¼ cup sugar
1½ tablespoons apricot liqueur or brandy
a big pinch of fresh thyme leaves

deep, 18-cm/7-in. tart pan or springform cake pan
baking sheet, lined with greaseproof paper
piping bag fitted with a plain nozzle/tip

Serves 6–8

Make the Pâte à Sablé Breton the day before you want to bake the tart, following the instructions on page 15. Refrigerate overnight, still between the sheets of paper.

The next day, preheat the oven to 170°C (325°F) Gas 3.

Roll the chilled dough out on a lightly floured surface until about 18 cm/7 inches in diameter. Loosely wrap the dough around the rolling pin and transfer it to the prepared tart pan. Unravel the dough into the pan. You just want to line the base of the pan, not the sides, so cut off any excess pastry with a small, sharp knife.

Bake in the preheated oven for 25–30 minutes or until golden and risen. The middle will sink slightly as it cools, which is what we want.

For the apricot crumble
Put all the ingredients in a food processor and blitz until it clumps together into a ball. Wrap the dough in clingfilm/plastic wrap and freeze for 1 hour or until frozen through.

For the apricot compote
Take half the apricots and finely chop them. Pit the remaining apricots, cut into wedges and reserve for later.

Heat and melt the butter in a frying pan, then fry the finely chopped apricots. Add the sugar and heat until the sugar has melted and the apricots have caramelized.

Remove the pan from the heat and carefully add the liqueur. Shake the pan a little over the heat and stand back slightly. The steam from the pan will ignite and the alcohol will burn off – this is perfectly normal. Just don't add too much otherwise you'll singe your eyebrows – I've seen it happen!

Add the thyme – it will give a nice colour and unexpected flavour. Once the apricots begin to break down and the liquid has reduced, transfer to a bowl and allow to cool slightly, then blitz in a food processor to make a chunky compote.

Preheat the oven to 180°C (350°F) Gas 4.

Take the frozen apricot crumble dough out of the freezer and coarsely grate it onto the prepared baking sheet. Bake in the preheated oven for 15 minutes. Give it a stir occasionally to stop it melting together into one big cookie. Allow to cool completely.

To serve, spoon the apricot compote into the naturally sunken base of the cooled tart case.

Fill the piping bag with Crème Diplomate and pipe bulbs in concentric circles between the compote filling and the edge of the tart case. Decorate with the reserved apricot wedges and sprinkle the crumble over the top. Finish with a dusting of icing/confectioners' sugar.

Prune and Armagnac tartlets

Armagnac is a distinctive kind of brandy produced in the region of the same name in Gascony, southwest France. Prunes soaked in Armagnac are one of those fantastic French concoctions that work in perfect harmony, and when you add soft, rich almond frangipane and crumbly pastry, you have got a match made in heaven. This flavour combination works exceptionally well at Christmas when you are sitting next to a roaring fire with a strong drink.

Soaked prunes

100 ml/½ cup Armagnac brandy
juice and grated zest of 1 orange
1 cinnamon stick
1 teaspoon mixed spice/apple pie spice
1-cm/½-inch fresh ginger, peeled and chopped
150 g/¾ cup soft, pitted prunes

Tartlet cases

1 x quantity Pâte Sucrée (page 12)
1 x quantity Frangipane (page 29)
grated zest of 2 lemons
3 tablespoons flaked/slivered almonds
icing/confectioners' sugar, to dust

12 individual tartlet pans, greased and lightly dusted with flour

Makes 12

For the soaked prunes

It is best to start soaking the prunes at least 1 day in advance of baking the tartlets, or if possible, soak them several weeks in advance in a sterilized jar. Their flavour will improve immeasurably over time.

Put the Armagnac, orange juice and zest, cinnamon stick, mixed spice/apple pie spice and ginger in a saucepan and bring to the boil.

Put the prunes in a heatproof bowl, pour the hot soaking liquid over them and allow to cool completely. Cover the bowl with clingfilm/plastic wrap and allow to soak overnight.

For the tartlet cases

When you are ready to make the tartlets, take the Pâte Sucrée out of the fridge and divide it into 12 equal portions. Using a rolling pin, roll out each portion on a lightly floured surface to a rough circle slightly larger than the diameter of the tartlet pans.

Loosely wrap one portion of dough at a time around the rolling pin and transfer it to a prepared tartlet pan. Unravel the dough into the pan. Gently coax the dough neatly into the curves and angles of the pan, press lightly into the sides and cut off any excess with a small, sharp knife.

Put the tartlet pans on a baking sheet and refrigerate for 1 hour.

Make the Frangipane following the instructions on page 29 and stir in the lemon zest at the end.

Preheat the oven to 180°C (350°F) Gas 4.

Take about half of the prunes out of their soaking liquid and chop them finely. Leave the remaining prunes whole.

Remove the tartlet cases from the fridge.

Divide the chopped prunes between the tartlet cases, then spoon the frangipane over the top. Cover with the remaining, whole prunes, then sprinkle the almonds over the top.

Bake the tartlets in the preheated oven for 30 minutes depending on their thickness. Test if they are done by inserting a skewer in the middle (try not to go all the way through in case you damage the pastry on the bottom) – if it comes out clean, they are ready.

Allow to cool slightly before removing the tartlets from the pans. To serve, dust with icing/confectioners' sugar.

BOURBONNEUX
SES MACARONS
BENOIST ET FILS
ERIE PATISSERIE

BOURBONNEUX
SES MACARONS
BENOIST ET FILS
ERIE PATISSERIE

‘Petit four’, meaning ‘at a low oven temperature’, gave its name to the miniature treats of the eighteenth century which needed gentle baking, at a low temperature. Nowadays the term is used for sweet fingerfood of the type you might get after dinner with coffee, with cocktails or perhaps to accompany a serving of ice cream. They should be delicate, gone in one or two bites, and leave you wanting more. Think chocolate truffles, infinitely appealing macarons, teeny sablés biscuits and sticky portions of fruit jelly. If possible, they shouldn’t be too heavy or rich since they are invariably served alongside or after other dishes.

Petits fours

Apricot and ginger florentines

'Caramelized, fruity, chewy nuggets of goodness' is what an old customer of mine used to say when eating my florentines. They work well either small or large, entirely dipped in chocolate or simply drizzled with it. What's great about them is that you can really make them your own with any flavouring. I have chosen dried apricots and ginger to add a warming, fruity touch to this recipe – perfect for autumn. You could add dried or glacé/candied cherries and ground cloves; some chocolate chips for Christmas; or a little orange zest or semi-dried berries for the summer.

50 g/3 tablespoons butter
150 g/¾ cup raw cane sugar
1½ tablespoons honey
3 tablespoons plain/all-purpose flour
300 ml/1¼ cups double/heavy cream
200 g/2½ cups flaked/slivered almonds
175 g/6 oz. dried apricots, finely chopped
50 g/2 oz. glacé ginger, finely chopped
75 g/2½ oz. dark chocolate

2 x 12-hole muffin pans, greased and dusted with flour

Makes about 24

The day before you want to bake the florentines, put the butter, sugar and honey in a heavy-based saucepan over low heat. Stir until the sugar has almost dissolved. Add the flour and continue to stir over gentle heat until the mixture is smooth and comes away from the sides of the pan.

Remove from the heat and slowly beat in the cream until smooth.

Return the pan to the heat and stir in the almonds, apricots and ginger. Transfer to a bowl and refrigerate overnight to set.

The next day, preheat the oven to 190°C (375°F) Gas 5.

Drop teaspoonfuls of the mixture into the prepared muffin pans and flatten slightly with the back of the spoon.

Bake in the preheated oven for 8–9 minutes, or until the florentines have spread and are bubbling and lightly browned at the edges. Remove from the oven and allow to cool for a couple of minutes, then flip them out of the pans with a small palette knife and allow to cool on a wire rack.

Melt the chocolate on low power in a microwave or in a heatproof bowl over a pan of simmering water (not letting the base of the bowl touch the water).

Decorate the florentines by dipping a spoon or fork into the melted chocolate and flicking it backwards and forwards over them.

Honey and vanilla madeleines

This is the kind of little romantic cake that the French do best. I can remember eating them for the first time when we went on a family holiday to Paris – I couldn't believe a cake this small and unassuming could be so moist and delicious! The moistness comes from the 'beurre noisette' (butter, melted and cooked until nut-brown) and ground almonds which release their natural oils when baked. One of the loveliest things about madeleines are their unique, delicate shell shape, so buy a special madeleine pan if you can!

125 g/1 stick butter
100 g/¾ cup icing/ confectioners' sugar
40 g/⅓ cup ground almonds
40 g/⅓ cup plain/ all-purpose flour
a pinch of salt
3 large egg whites
2 teaspoons honey
grated zest of 2 lemons
1 teaspoon vanilla extract

piping bag fitted with a plain nozzle/tip (optional)
12-hole madeleine pan, well greased and lightly dusted with flour

Makes 12

Put the butter in a saucepan over medium heat and allow to melt. Continue to cook until it turns golden brown – this is called a 'beurre noisette', ie butter the colour of nuts. It gives madeleines their deep golden colour and distinctive nutty flavour. When the butter has turned the right colour and stopped sizzling, it is ready. Remove from the heat and allow to cool completely.

Sift the sugar, almonds, flour and salt into a mixing bowl. Whisk in the egg whites, honey, lemon zest and vanilla using a balloon whisk.

Finally, whisk in the cooled beurre noisette.

Cover the bowl with clingfilm/plastic wrap and refrigerate for 30–40 minutes. This will help achieve the right texture.

Pipe or spoon the mixture into the madeleine pan, then refrigerate again for 20 minutes to help make a firm skin when the madeleines are baked.

Preheat the oven to 170°C (325°F) Gas 3.

Bake the madeleines in the preheated oven for 10–15 minutes.

Allow to cool completely in the pan.

These are perfect with a little chocolate dipping sauce, or dipped into a mid-morning cup of coffee or hot chocolate!

Coffee and chocolate madeleines

These are less innocent versions of classic madeleines (page 91), best made with really good coffee and even better unsweetened cocoa powder. Put them in a cellophane gift bag and give them to friends and family at Christmas time. For an extra dose of indulgence, I half-dip them in chocolate and dust them in coffee – irresistible!

125 g/1 stick butter
100 g/¾ cup icing/confectioners' sugar
30 g/⅓ cup ground almonds
30 g/¼ cup plain/all-purpose flour
1½ tablespoons cocoa powder
a pinch of salt
1½ tablespoons instant coffee granules, plus extra, ground, to dust
3 large egg whites
2 teaspoons honey
1 teaspoon vanilla extract
250 g/9 oz. dark Tempered Chocolate (page 33)

piping bag fitted with a plain nozzle/tip (optional)
12-hole madeleine pan, well greased and lightly dusted with flour

Makes 12

Put the butter in a saucepan over medium heat and allow to melt. Continue to cook until it turns golden brown – this is called a 'beurre noisette', ie butter the colour of nuts. It gives madeleines their deep golden colour and distinctive nutty flavour. When the butter has turned the right colour and stopped sizzling, it is ready. Remove from the heat and allow it to cool completely.

Sift the sugar, almonds, flour, cocoa powder and salt into a mixing bowl. Whisk in the coffee granules, egg whites, honey and vanilla using a balloon whisk.

Finally, whisk in the cooled beurre noisette.

Cover the bowl with clingfilm/plastic wrap and refrigerate for 30–40 minutes. This will help achieve the right texture.

Pipe or spoon the mixture into the madeleine pan, then refrigerate again for 20 minutes to help make a firm skin when the madeleines are baked.

Preheat the oven to 170°C (325°F) Gas 3.

Bake the madeleines in the preheated oven for 10–15 minutes.

Allow to cool completely in the pan.

Dip half of each madeleine in the Tempered Chocolate and dust a little finely ground instant coffee granules over the top. Allow to set before serving.

White chocolate and almond truffles

White chocolate can often be overly sweet, but I find that rolling these simple truffles in roasted almonds tempers the sweetness and stops them being too cloying. The chopped nuts serve to add great texture too. I have piped them into little logs but you could just as easily roll them into balls between your hands, or shape them roughly like little rocks.

100 ml/scant ½ cup whipping cream
2 tablespoons butter
a pinch of salt
550 g/1 lb. 2 oz. white chocolate, chopped
250 g/2 cups blanched almonds

piping bag fitted with a 2-cm/¾-in. plain nozzle/tip

Makes about 24

Put the cream, butter and salt in a saucepan and bring to the boil over low heat.

Pour the boiled cream into a heatproof bowl and add 250 g/9 oz. of the chocolate. Using a spatula, start to mix the ingredients in a circular motion, just in the centre of the bowl. Keep mixing in a tight circle until the chocolate starts to melt and emulsify with the liquid. Gradually widen the circle until all the chocolate has melted and you have a shiny, smooth ganache.

If the ganache looks like it is splitting, add a dash of cold milk – that should bring it back.

Refrigerate the ganache for about 1 hour, giving it a quick whisk every 15 minutes to speed up the cooling process.

Fill a piping bag with the ganache and pipe long logs onto a sheet of greaseproof paper.

Refrigerate and allow to set completely.

Meanwhile, preheat the oven to 180°C (350°F) Gas 4.

Put the almonds on a baking sheet and roast in the preheated oven for a few minutes, stirring halfway through, until lightly toasted.

Allow the almonds to cool completely, then finely chop them.

Melt the remaining chocolate on low power in a microwave or in a heatproof bowl over a pan of simmering water (not letting the base of the bowl touch the water).

Transfer the chilled logs of chocolate to a chopping/cutting board and cut into 5-cm/2-inch lengths.

Have the following ready: the bowl of melted chocolate; the toasted almonds on a plate; and a sheet of greaseproof paper.

Dip and roll the truffles in the melted chocolate, fish out with a fork, then roll them in the nuts. Allow to set on the greaseproof paper.

VARIATIONS

Passionfruit: Replace half the cream with strained passionfruit pulp.

Orange: add the grated zest of 1 orange to the cream for a little orange backnote.

Celebration: Roll the truffles in crushed freeze-dried blackcurrants and edible glitter, instead of the chopped almonds, for a shimmery purple coating ideally suited to a party.

Orange and Cointreau chocolate truffles

Chocolate and orange are a well-loved pairing. Add a little Cointreau liqueur to the equation and you have got an altogether more adult concoction that is perfectly suited to scrumptious little truffles. Of course, you could replace the liqueur with orange juice if any children are likely to want to enjoy these too. If you can easily find it, I urge you to include the mandarin olive oil which adds an amazing depth of flavour and assists in making the ganache so silky.

100 ml/scant ½ cup whipping cream
3 tablespoons Cointreau liqueur
grated zest of 1 orange
1 tablespoon mandarin olive oil (available online)
2 tablespoons orange blossom honey
175 g/6 oz. dark chocolate (65% cocoa), chopped
cocoa powder, to dust (optional)

piping bag fitted with a plain nozzle/tip

Makes 20–30

Put the cream, Cointreau, orange zest, olive oil and honey in a saucepan and bring to the boil over low heat.

Remove from the heat, cover with clingfilm/ plastic wrap and allow to infuse for 1 hour.

Put the infused cream back on the heat and bring gently to the boil again. Pour through a sieve/strainer and into a heatproof bowl, then add the chocolate.

Using a spatula, start to mix the ingredients in a circular motion, just in the centre of the bowl. Keep mixing in a tight circle until the chocolate starts to melt and emulsify with the liquid. Gradually widen the circle until all the chocolate has melted and you have a shiny, smooth ganache.

If the ganache looks like it is splitting, add a dash of cold milk – that should bring it back.

Allow to cool for 30–45 minutes, or until it is firm enough to pipe. Give it a quick whisk every 15 minutes to speed up the cooling process.

Fill the piping bag with the ganache and pipe bulbs onto a sheet of greaseproof paper. Dust with cocoa powder, if you like, and allow to set.

VARIATIONS

Blackcurrant and cassis: omit the orange zest, olive oil and honey; replace the Cointreau with just 2 tablespoons crème de cassis liqueur; replace the cream with blackcurrant purée (page 112); and increase the chocolate to 200 g/7 oz.

Apple and Calvados: omit the orange zest, olive oil and honey; replace the Cointreau with just 2 tablespoons Calvados liqueur; replace half the cream with apple compote (page 44, blended until smooth); and increase the chocolate to 100 g/3½ oz. each milk and dark chocolate.

Raspberry and Framboise: omit the orange zest, olive oil and honey; replace the Cointreau with just 2 tablespoons Framboise liqueur; replace the cream with raspberry purée (page 99); and increase the chocolate to 200 g/7 oz.

Praline and Amaretto: omit the orange zest, olive oil and honey; replace the Cointreau with just 2 tablespoons Amaretto; increase the chocolate to 100 g/3½ oz. each milk and dark chocolate; and add 1 tablespoon praline paste (available online).

Raspberry and vodka chocolate truffles

These pretty chocolate truffles are perfect in the summer with a glass of Champagne. Unlike the traditional cream-based ganache, this is made with raspberry purée and uses olive oil instead of butter, so it is dairy free. You can buy great raspberry purée online or in really good supermarkets, but it is so easy to make your own – see below. You could also just use water instead of the vodka and olive oil for a very clean chocolate flavour – this is a trendy technique at the moment. This still-warm ganache can also be used as a chocolate sauce.

250 g/9 oz. dark Tempered Chocolate (page 33)
freeze-dried raspberry powder (available online), to coat

Raspberry purée
200 g/1½ cups raspberries
juice of 1 lemon
1 tablespoon icing/ confectioners' sugar

Truffle ganache
3 tablespoons vodka
a pinch of salt
1 tablespoon olive oil
200 g/7 oz. dark chocolate, chopped

piping bag fitted with a 2-cm/¾-in. plain nozzle/tip

Makes about 24

For the raspberry purée
Put the raspberries, lemon juice and sugar in a blender or food processor and blitz until smooth. Pass the purée through a sieve/strainer to make it extra smooth.

For the truffle ganache
Put the raspberry purée and vodka in a saucepan and bring to the boil over low heat.

Pour the boiled mixture into a heatproof bowl and add the dark chocolate. Using a spatula, start to mix the ingredients in a circular motion, just in the centre of the bowl. Keep mixing in a tight circle until the chocolate starts to melt and emulsify with the liquid. Gradually widen the circle until all the chocolate has melted and you have a shiny, smooth ganache.

If the ganache looks like it is splitting, add a dash of cold milk – that should bring it back.

Allow to cool for 30–45 minutes, or until it is firm enough to pipe. Give it a quick whisk every 15 minutes to speed up the cooling process.

Fill a piping bag with the ganache and pipe long logs onto a sheet of greaseproof paper.

Refrigerate and allow to set completely.

Transfer the chilled logs of chocolate onto a chopping/cutting board and cut into 5-cm/ 2-inch lengths.

Have the following ready: the bowl of Tempered Chocolate; the freeze-dried raspberry powder on a plate; and a sheet of greaseproof paper.

Dip and roll the truffles in the tempered chocolate, fish out with a fork, then roll them in the raspberry powder. Allow to set on the greaseproof paper.

Cherry and Kirsch chocolate truffles

As you can probably tell from the Gâteaux and Desserts chapter of the book later on, I love Black Forest gâteau in any form. So it follows that I had to create a chocolate truffle that tastes and looks like this beloved cake of mine.

250 g/9 oz. dark Tempered Chocolate (page 33)
175 g/6 oz. dark or milk chocolate, finely grated

Cherry purée
500 g/1 lb. cherries, pitted and halved
25 g/2 tablespoons sugar
juice of 1 orange

Truffle ganache
50 ml/¼ cup whipping cream
3 tablespoons Kirsch liqueur
1 tablespoon salted butter
2 tablespoons honey or glucose syrup
90 g/3 oz. dark chocolate (70% cocoa), chopped
90 g/3 oz. milk chocolate, chopped

Makes 20–30

For the cherry purée
Put the cherries, sugar and orange juice in a saucepan over medium heat. Bring to the boil, then cook for a further 10 minutes.

Allow to cool slightly, then transfer to a blender or food processor and process until smooth. Add a dash of water to make it runnier if you prefer. Pass the purée through a sieve/strainer to make it extra smooth.

For the truffle ganache
Put the cream, 50 ml/¼ cup of the cherry purée, the Kirsch, butter and honey or glucose in a saucepan and bring to the boil over low heat.

Pour the boiled mixture into a heatproof bowl and add the dark and milk chocolates. Using a spatula, start to mix the ingredients in a circular motion, just in the centre of the bowl. Keep mixing in a tight circle until the chocolate starts to melt and emulsify with the liquid. Gradually widen the circle until all the chocolate has melted and you have a shiny, smooth ganache.

If the ganache looks like it is splitting, add a dash of cold milk – that should bring it back.

Refrigerate and allow to set completely.

Scoop out a teaspoon at a time of the chilled ganache and roll between your hands to make a smooth ball.

Have the following ready: the bowl of Tempered Chocolate; the grated chocolate on a plate; and a sheet of greaseproof paper.

Dip and roll the truffles in the tempered chocolate, fish out with a fork, then roll them in the grated chocolate. Allow to set on the greaseproof paper.

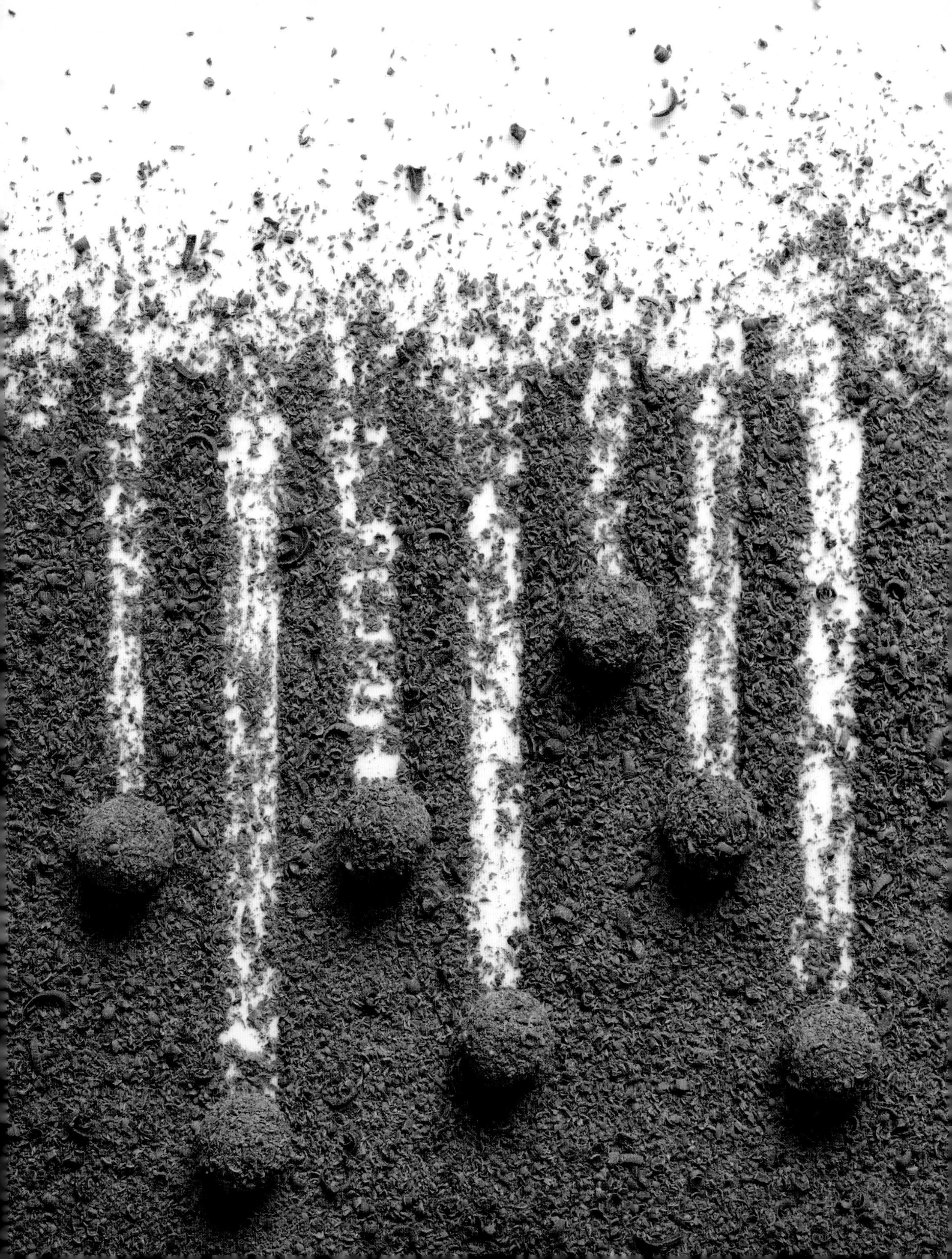

Passionfruit, mango and olive oil chocolates

I love to give traditional chocolates a twist by making them with fruit purées and olive oil. This particular tropical explosion tops a wonderfully crunchy sesame-seed base that has an extra little surprise when you bite into it – popping candy! It's fun and kids will love it. I made a very similar version of this for a really good friend's wedding this year and seeing the guests' faces when they ate the chocolates was priceless. Grown men and women were reduced to childish laughter reminiscing about years gone by and experiences with space dust!

250 g/9 oz. dark Tempered Chocolate (page 33)

Base

100 g/3½ oz. milk chocolate
100 g/6 tablespoons tahini paste
50 ml/3 tablespoons extra virgin olive oil
40 g/¼ cup black sesame seeds
140 g/5 oz. chocolate popping candy (available online)

Ganache

250 ml/1 cup mango and passionfruit smoothie
juice of 2 passionfruit, strained
1½ tablespoons extra virgin olive oil
350 g/12 oz. dark chocolate (Grenada origin, 66% cocoa, if you can find it), chopped

15-cm/6-in. square frame

Makes about 25

Start the recipe the day before you want to serve the truffles.

For the base

Melt the milk chocolate and tahini paste in a heatproof bowl over a pan of simmering water (not letting the base of the bowl touch the water).

Allow to cool and thicken slightly, then add the olive oil, sesame seeds and popping candy.

Spread the mixture out on a sheet of greaseproof paper and top with another sheet. Roll it thinly with a rolling pin, then refrigerate to set, still between the sheets of paper.

Remove the chilled mixture from the fridge, remove the top sheet of paper and place the square frame over it. Press the frame down to cut all the way through the mixture, then leave the frame pressed in place.

For the ganache

Put the passionfruit and mango smoothie, passionfruit juice and olive oil in a saucepan and bring to the boil over low heat.

Pour the boiled mixture into a heatproof bowl and add the chocolate. Using a spatula, start to mix the ingredients in a circular motion, just in the centre of the bowl. Keep mixing in a tight circle until the chocolate starts to melt and emulsify with the liquid. Gradually widen the circle until all the chocolate has melted and you have a shiny, smooth ganache.

If the ganache looks like it is splitting, add a dash of cold milk – that should bring it back.

Pour the ganache into the frame over the crunchy base. Allow to set at room temperature overnight.

The next day, gently ease the frame away from the chocolate. Cut it into 5 rows of 5 squares each using a large, sharp knife.

Dip the chocolate squares in the Tempered Chocolate with a dipping fork or regular fork and set on a sheet of greaseproof paper.

To create that professional pattern on top, lay the three prongs of the fork flat on top of each chocolate and when you lift the fork up again, drag it to the right. The melted chocolate will fall into that distinctive pattern. Allow to set.

Apple pie and custard chocolate tartlets

When I was little, my Nans used to make the most amazing apple pies, always served with custard of course! So I developed the recipe to take me back to my childhood: apple compote, caramel chocolate and custard. I wanted to get that cooked pastry taste into the mix so I asked my good friend and culinary mentor Heston Blumenthal about it and he suggested adding a pinch of dried yeast to the crème anglaise filling – not very French, but this one's for my Nans!

½ quantity Pâte Sablée (page 12)
200 g/7 oz. caramel chocolate (available online), chopped
1½ tablespoons butter
125 g/½ cup Apple Compote (page 44)
edible gold leaf, to decorate

Crème anglaise
125 ml/½ cup milk
125 ml/½ cup whipping cream
1 teaspoon vanilla extract
3 egg yolks
2 tablespoons caster/ superfine sugar
1 teaspoon dried yeast
2 tablespoons Calvados liqueur

24-hole mini-muffin pan, greased and lightly dusted with flour
baking beans

Makes about 15

Preheat the oven to 170°C (325°F) Gas 3.

Take the Pâte Sablée out of the fridge and put on a lightly floured surface. Using a rolling pin, roll it out until 5 mm/¼ inch thick. Find a glass with a diameter about the same as the top of each hole in the muffin pan. Stamp out about 15 rounds and lay them in the bases of the muffin pan holes. Gently press them in to get a neat case with a rim around the edge.

Lay a small piece of greaseproof paper over each pan and fill it with baking beans. Bake in the preheated oven for about 10–15 minutes.

For the crème anglaise

Put the milk, cream and vanilla in a saucepan and bring to the boil over low heat.

Meanwhile, in a bowl, whisk together the egg yolks and sugar until pale.

Pour the boiled cream mixture very gradually into the mixing bowl, whisking all the time to prevent the egg yolks from cooking into lumps.

Return the mixture to the pan over very low heat and cook, stirring all the time, until creamy and it coats the back of a wooden spoon when you dip it in.

Measure out 100 ml/½ cup of the crème anglaise (keep the remainder in an airtight container to serve with dessert in the next couple of days).

Put the dried yeast and Calvados in a small saucepan over low heat and warm just until the yeast has dissolved. Stir into the hot crème anglaise, then pour this into a heatproof bowl. Add the caramel chocolate and butter. Using a spatula, start to mix the ingredients in a circular motion, just in the centre of the bowl. Keep mixing in a tight circle until the chocolate starts to melt and emulsify with the liquid. Gradually widen the circle until all the chocolate has melted and you have a shiny, smooth ganache.

If the ganache looks like it is splitting, add a dash of cold milk – that should bring it back.

Remove the paper and beans from the tartlet cases and pop them out of the pan and onto a tray. Divide the apple compote between the tartlet cases and pour the ganache over the top. Allow to cool slightly, then garnish with a smidgen of gold leaf.

Allow to cool completely before serving.

Macarons

175 g/1¾ cups ground almonds
175 g/1½ cups icing/confectioners' sugar
50 g/scant ¼ cup egg whites (1–2 egg whites)
100 g/scant ½ cup egg whites (about 3 egg whites)
200 g/1 cup caster/superfine sugar
1 teaspoon vanilla extract

cookie cutter, about 4 cm/1½ in.
large piping bag fitted with a plain nozzle/tip
baking sheets, lined with greaseproof paper

Makes about 30

I couldn't write this book without featuring the most fashionable thing to come out of France for decades. Macarons are one of those things that can break people, as they can so easily go wrong, but they have become so popular and trendy in the last few years that you just have to give them a go. Although things can go wrong, once you master the technique, it is so satisfying to put your own twist on them. By tinting the mixture different colours, you can match the filling with the shell, and if you want to go one step further, you can add freeze-dried flavourings, like I have here – they are available online.

Before you start the recipe, take the cookie cutter and a sheet of paper or card. Draw around the cutter to make rows of circles on the paper, leaving a bit of space in between. This will be your template to ensure perfect macarons that are all the same size. **(A)**

Put the ground almonds and icing/confectioners' sugar in a food processor and process to a fine powder. (If you are making pistachio macarons, replace one-third of the ground almonds with ground pistachios at this stage.) Transfer to a mixing bowl with the 50 g/scant ¼ cup egg whites and beat together with a spatula until it becomes paste-like. Set aside for later. **(B)**

Put the 100 g/scant ½ cup egg whites in a separate, heatproof bowl and whisk with an electric whisk until soft peaks form.

Get a small–medium saucepan ready on the heat with a shallow depth of simmering water.

Raspberry macarons

1 tablespoon freeze-dried raspberry powder (available online)

pink food colouring paste (optional)

finely chopped dried raspberries, to decorate

Pistachio macarons

replace 60 g/⅔ cup of the ground almonds with ground pistachios

green food colouring paste (optional)

finely chopped pistachios, to decorate

Coffee macarons

2 teaspoons instant coffee granules, ground, plus extra to decorate

1 tablespoon coffee extract

Mango macarons

1 tablespoon freeze-dried mango powder (available online)

yellow food colouring paste (optional)

Set the bowl on top of the saucepan, making sure the bottom of the bowl doesn't touch the water. Add the sugar to the egg whites and continue to whisk until it starts to increase in volume again. **(C)**

Now remove the bowl from the heat and continue to whisk with the electric whisk, or transfer the mixture to a stand mixer. Whisk until thick, glossy and cool. **(D)**

Add the vanilla. Gently fold in the reserved almond mixture with a large metal spoon, being careful not to over-mix.

At this point, you can add your chosen flavourings and colourings. See left for ingredients to make rapsberry, pistachio, coffee and mango macarons. Add the chosen flavourings and a couple of dots of food colouring paste to boost the colour, if you like. Fold in until evenly incorporated.

Slip your template between the prepared paper and baking sheet. Fill a piping bag with the mixture and pipe rounds onto the paper with the template to guide you. Gently pull the template out after you have finished. **(E)**

Set aside for 30–60 minutes to firm up and form a slight skin.

Preheat the oven to 160°C (325°F) Gas 3.

Sprinkle any chosen decorations on top of the macarons if you like, but not too much otherwise they won't rise nicely when baking.

Bake the macarons in the preheated oven with the oven door slightly ajar for 10–12 minutes, keeping an eye on them in case they are browning too quickly.

Remove from the oven and allow to cool completely on the sheets.

To fill, use one of the suggestions below, or try Crème Diplomate (page 26) or just jam. **(F)**

To fill raspberry macarons

Make a ganache following the instructions on page 30 but use 50 ml/¼ cup raspberry purée or juice instead of the cream, and 100 g/3½ oz. dark chocolate. Allow to set slightly before piping onto the flat side of half of the macarons and sandwiching with the other half.

To fill pistachio macarons

Make a ganache following the instructions on page 30 but use 50 ml/3 tablespoons whipping cream with 2 tablespoons pistachio paste (available online or see page 79) instead of the pure cream, and 50 g/2 oz. each dark and milk chocolate. Allow to set slightly before piping onto the flat side of half of the macarons and sandwiching with the other half.

To fill coffee macarons

Make a ganache following the instructions on page 30 but use 3 tablespoons whipping cream with 2 teaspoons espresso and 1 teaspoon instant coffee granules, and 100 g/3½ oz. dark chocolate (75% cocoa). Allow to set slightly before piping onto the flat side of half of the macarons and sandwiching with the other half.

To fill mango macarons

Make a ganache following the instructions on page 30 but use 2 tablespoons mango purée with 2 tablespoons passionfruit purée and 2 teaspoons butter, and 150 g/5½ oz. white chocolate. Allow to set slightly before piping onto the flat side of half of the macarons and sandwiching with the other half.

C

D

E

F

Almond and honey friands

These buttery little fancies are perfect at the end of a meal or with a little cup of espresso for elevenses! You can make the mixture ahead of time and store it in the fridge to bake when needed. I sometimes ring the changes and flavour these with finely ground Earl Grey tea leaves and lemon zest, then eat them straight from the oven with a lovely cup of Earl Grey tea. Just be careful though – they are seriously addictive!

6 egg whites
75 g/½ cup plain/ all-purpose flour
250 g/1¾ cups icing/ confectioners' sugar
125 g/1¼ cups ground almonds
2 tablespoons honey
½ teaspoon almond extract
grated zest of 1 lemon
175 g/12 tablespoons butter, melted and cooled

12-hole friand or muffin pan, greased

Makes 12

Preheat the oven to 200°C (400°F) Gas 6.

Put the egg whites in a stand mixer or in a bowl using an electric whisk and whisk until frothy.

Sift the flour, sugar, and almonds into a mixing bowl.

Add the egg whites, honey, almond extract, lemon zest to the mixing bowl, then pour in the cooled, melted butter. Beat until well blended.

Divide the mixture between the holes of the friand pan, filling them no more than three-quarters full.

Bake the friands in the preheated oven for 20–22 minutes, or until risen and lightly golden around the edges.

Remove from the oven and allow to cool in the pan for about 5 minutes.

To tip them out, turn the whole pan upside down on a clean surface and tap it until the friands drop out. Transfer to a wire rack to cool.

Devour these tiny treats with strong coffee.

VARIATION

Make a double batch of these friands and use some at the bottom of a trifle, doused with your favourite tipple and covered with fresh fruit, Crème Pâtissière (page 25) and Crème Chantilly (page 26).

Cassis pâte de fruit

These little sugary jellies are classic French petits fours and can be found all over the world in various guises. They are delicious as after-dinner delicacies and work in so many different flavours. I find that sharp flavours such as passionfruit and blackcurrant work particularly well. Once they are coated in sugar and look so pretty, consider packing them in small cellophane bags to give as special, handmade gifts.

1 big teaspoon pectin
40 g/3 tablespoons sugar
280 g/1½ cups sugar, plus extra, to dust
140 g/generous ½ cup glucose syrup
120 ml/½ cup water
a dash of crème de cassis liqueur

Blackcurrant purée
200 g/2 cups frozen blackcurrants
juice of 1 lemon
1 tablespoon icing/confectioners' sugar

sugar thermometer
deep, 30 x 25-cm/12 x 10-in. baking pan, lined with greaseproof paper

Makes about 30

Start the recipe the day before you want to serve the jellies.

For the blackcurrant purée
Put the blackcurrants, lemon juice and sugar in a blender or food processor and blitz until smooth. Pass the purée through a sieve/strainer to make it extra smooth.

Put the blackcurrant purée in a large saucepan over medium heat and bring to the boil.

In a small bowl, mix together the pectin and the 40 g/3 tablespoons sugar.

Put the 280 g/1½ cups sugar, the glucose, water and cassis liqueur in a separate saucepan over medium heat and heat until it comes to the boil.

Sprinkle the pectin mixture into the pan of boiling blackcurrant purée, then add the warm glucose mixture.

Bring to the boil and keep boiling until the mixture reads 114°C/237°F on a sugar thermometer. Stir constantly to prevent the mixture from burning.

When it is ready, pour it into the prepared baking pan and allow to set overnight.

The next day, cut the set jelly into squares and coat in sugar.

For an extra hit of fruit, you could add freeze-dried blackcurrant powder to the sugar for coating the jellies.

Sesame and poppy seed tuiles

When I was training at the University of West London, my work placement in my first year was at The Dorchester, one of London's most famous hotels. I was in awe of the amazing afternoon-tea pastries and desserts! I remember having to make hundreds of sesame tuiles and being surprised how easy they were to make and how versatile they could be. Place a hot tuile, straight from the oven, over a ladle to make a basket for ice cream and fruit – an edible bowl – or make curved discs like I have to serve as a light petit four.

250 g/2 cups icing/ confectioners' sugar
75 g/⅔ cup plain/ all-purpose flour
150 ml/⅔ cup water
125 g/1 stick butter, melted
30 g/¼ cup white sesame seeds
30 g/¼ cup poppy seeds

bent or 'step' palette knife (optional)
silicone mat, or baking sheet lined with greaseproof paper

Makes 20–30

Sift the sugar and flour into a mixing bowl.

Pour the water and melted butter into the bowl and whisk with a balloon whisk until evenly combined.

Stir in the sesame and poppy seeds.

Allow the mixture to rest and set for 1–2 hours.

When you are ready to bake the tuiles, preheat the oven to 190°C (375°F) Gas 5.

It is best to use a bent or 'step' palette knife for this next stage but a spoon would do. Drop a spoonful of the mixture onto the silicone mat or prepared baking sheet and spread it thinly into a disc using the palette knife or the back of a spoon. Repeat with the remaining mixture.

Bake in the preheated oven for 10 minutes.

Remove the tuiles from the oven and lift each one up with a spatula, then drape it over a rolling pin – it will be pliable enough to bend over the rolling pin but it will cool and firm up very quickly so work as swiftly as you can. Set the shaped tuiles on a sheet of greaseproof paper to cool completely.

If you find the rest of the freshly baked tuiles are setting too fast while you work, put them back in the warm oven for a few seconds to soften again.

Alternatively, you can drape the tuiles over an upturned soup ladle to create a basket shape.

Serve the tuiles on their own as petits fours after dinner, or as an accompaniment to desserts such as ice cream.

Langues de chat

These delicate little cookies translate as 'cats' tongues'. They take just moments to rustle up and once you get the hang of them, you probably won't need to make yourself a template to make perfect shapes every time. They are the ideal partner to a very strong coffee in the morning, Parisian style! Originating in the seventeenth century, they are also found in German and Austrian pâtisseries and bakeries, often enrobed in dark or milk chocolate. I have added almonds to mine to add extra flavour and texture.

100 g/¾ cup icing/ confectioners' sugar
100 g/6½ tablespoons butter, softened
1 teaspoon vanilla extract
2 large egg whites
100 g/¾ cup plain/ all-purpose flour
60 g/½ cup ground almonds
25 g/3 tablespoons flaked/slivered almonds

piping bag fitted with a plain nozzle/tip
baking sheet, lined with greaseproof paper

Makes about 24

Preheat the oven to 200°C (400°F) Gas 6.

Before you start the recipe, take a sheet of paper or card. Draw equal ovals about 7 cm/ 3 inches long to make rows of ovals on the paper, leaving a bit of space in between. This will be your template to ensure perfect cookies that are all the same size.

Put the sugar, butter and vanilla in a mixing bowl and beat with a wooden spoon until fluffy.

Beat in the egg whites, one at a time.

Gently fold in the flour and ground almonds with a large metal spoon.

Slip your template between the prepared paper and baking sheet. Fill a piping bag with the mixture and pipe ovals onto the paper with the template to guide you. Gently pull the template out after you have finished.

Sprinkle the flaked/slivered almonds over the cookies.

Bake in the preheated oven for about 8 minutes until starting to turn golden at the edges.

Remove from the oven and allow to cool for a couple of minutes, then transfer to a wire rack to cool completely.

Serve them just as they are, or sandwich them together with a spoonful of Ganache (page 30) or apricot jam.

Chocolate and hazelnut sablés

Everyone loves chocolate cookies, especially if they are dipped in chocolate or filled with chocolate buttercream. I have a soft spot for chocolate and hazelnut together, so I make these sablés with ground hazelnuts, dip them in dark chocolate and sprinkle them with roasted hazelnuts and grué de cacao (cocoa nibs), which lends a deep, bitter chocolate burst.

75 g/scant ⅔ cup icing/confectioners' sugar
150 g/11 tablespoons butter, softened
1 vanilla bean
grated zest of 1 orange
2 eggs, lightly beaten
200 g/1¾ cups plain/all-purpose flour
50 g/½ cup ground hazelnuts
2 tablespoons cocoa powder
250 g/9 oz. dark Tempered Chocolate (page 33)
3 tablespoons hazelnuts
3 tablespoons grué de cacao/cocoa nibs (available online)

cookie cutter, about 4 cm/1½ in. in diameter
non-stick baking sheet, lightly dusted with flour

Makes 20–25

Put the sugar and butter in a mixing bowl and beat with a wooden spoon until pale and fluffy.

Split the vanilla bean lengthwise using a small, sharp knife and scrape the seeds out into the bowl. Add the orange zest and beat in.

Gradually beat in the eggs until well incorporated. Gently fold in the flour, ground hazelnuts and cocoa powder with a large metal spoon, but do not over-work the dough otherwise the gluten will develop and you will end up with sablés that are tough rather than crisp and light.

Bring the dough together into a ball with your hands, wrap in clingfilm/plastic wrap and refrigerate until needed – about 1 hour.

When you are ready to bake the sablés, preheat the oven to 170°C (325°F) Gas 3.

Take the dough out of the fridge and put on a lightly floured surface. Using a rolling pin, roll it out until about 5 mm/¼ inch thick.

Stamp out rounds with the cookie cutter and arrange on the prepared baking sheet.

Bake in the preheated oven for 10 minutes.

Remove the sablés from the oven and allow to cool completely on the baking sheet. Leave the oven on.

Put the hazelnuts on a baking sheet and roast in the hot oven for a few minutes, stirring halfway through, until lightly toasted.

Allow the hazelnuts to cool slightly, then finely chop them.

Dip half of each sablé in the Tempered Chocolate and sprinkle the chopped hazelnuts and grué de cacao over the top. Allow to set before serving.

These will keep for about 2 weeks in an airtight container, should you be able to resist them for that long…

VARIATIONS

Orange: mix 1 tablespoon icing/confectioners' sugar with 2–3 teaspoons freshly squeezed orange juice. Drizzle it over the baked sablés instead of dipping them in chocolate.

Pistachio and raspberry: replace the ground almonds and cocoa powder with ground pistachios. Drizzle melted white chocolate over the baked sablés instead of dipping them in chocolate and sprinkle chopped freeze-dried raspberries over the top.

Cinnamon, orange and clove sablés

As a child, I used to visit family friends from Chicago, especially around Christmas time. They and my parents drank mulled wine (with a lot of brandy, I seem to remember) and sat around the piano while my sister and I were enamoured by those prickly oranges sitting on radiators giving off an incredible scent of orange and cloves. I think this is where my love for this flavour combination comes from. To this day, I still make some at Christmas to remind me of my childhood: I stud oranges with cloves in ornate patterns, tie them with ribbon and cinnamon sticks and sit them on warm radiators.

75 g/scant ⅔ cup icing/confectioners' sugar, plus extra to dust
150 g/11 tablespoons butter, softened
1 vanilla bean
grated zest of 2 oranges
2 eggs, lightly beaten
250 g/2 cups plain/all-purpose flour
1 teaspoon ground cinnamon
½ teaspoon ground cloves

assorted star-shaped cookie cutters
non-stick baking sheet, lightly dusted with flour

Makes 20–25

Put the sugar and butter in a mixing bowl and beat with a wooden spoon until pale and fluffy.

Split the vanilla bean lengthwise using a small, sharp knife and scrape the seeds out into the bowl. Add the orange zest and beat in.

Gradually beat in the eggs until well incorporated. Gently fold in the flour, cinnamon and cloves with a large metal spoon, but do not over-work the dough otherwise the gluten will develop and you will end up with sablés that are tough rather than crisp and light.

Bring the dough together into a ball with your hands, wrap in clingfilm/plastic wrap and refrigerate until needed – about 1 hour.

When you are ready to bake the sablés, preheat the oven to 170°C (325°F) Gas 3.

Take the dough out of the fridge and put on a lightly floured surface. Using a rolling pin, roll it out until about 5 mm/¼ inch thick.

Stamp out stars with the cookie cutters and arrange on the prepared baking sheet.

Bake in the preheated oven for 10 minutes.

Remove the sablés from the oven and allow to cool slightly on the baking sheet. Dust with icing/confectioners' sugar to serve. I like to eat them warm!

VARIATION

These sablés make lovely Christmas tree decorations. Before baking, use a skewer to gently push a hole through the stars, near the top. Bake as described above, then you might need to re-shape the holes if they have closed up too much. Thread a ribbon through them and hang the sablés on your Christmas tree.

Imagine a rich and complex cake – perhaps layered or featuring many pastry elements – filled with cream and fruit, chocolate and/or nuts, and you are probably calling to mind a gâteau. This is the opportunity you have been waiting for to put into practice some of the techniques you have learnt along your pâtisserie journey and assemble a cake that will have guests gasping with delight and applauding you for your new-found skills. Some of the offerings in this chapter fall into the category of desserts but they are likely to grace a French tea room or café menu, and may still make use of previously encountered pastry techniques.

Gâteaux and desserts

Chocolate and caramelized banana gâteau

One of my guilty pleasures has to be banoffee pie – the crunch of the base, sweetness of the caramel, softness and richness of the bananas and then the cream! To give it a French twist, I combine a layered mousse gâteau with the classic caramel and bananas. And there's a lovely cheat for the caramel too!

½ quantity Chocolate Almond Cake mixture (page 134)
400 g/14 oz. canned caramel or dulce de leche

Caramelized bananas
2 teaspoons butter
2 large bananas, sliced
50 g/¼ cup sugar

Chocolate mousse
2 sheets of gelatine
120 g/⅔ cup sugar
240 ml/1 cup whipping cream
560 ml/2⅓ cups whipping cream
200 g/7 oz. dark chocolate, chopped

Ganache topping
100 ml/½ cup whipping cream
1 tablespoon glucose syrup
1½ tablespoons butter
120 g/4 oz. dark and 80 g/3 oz. milk chocolate, chopped

Swiss/jelly roll pan, lined with greaseproof paper
deep, 20-cm/8-in. round springform cake pan, lined with greaseproof paper

Serves about 8

Start the recipe the day before you want to serve the cake. Preheat the oven to 190°C (375°F) Gas 5.

Make the Chocolate Almond Cake mixture following the instructions on page 134. Spread the mixture thinly and evenly into the prepared Swiss/jelly roll pan and bake in the preheated oven for 5–10 minutes. Flip the cake onto a sheet of greaseproof paper dusted with a little semolina. Peel the baking paper off the top and allow to cool.

Cut a circle out of the cooled cake using the round cake pan as a guide, but cut it about 2.5 cm/1 inch smaller than the pan. Put the cake circle inside the cake pan and spoon the canned caramel evenly over it.

For the caramelized bananas
Put a non-stick frying pan over medium heat, add the butter and briefly fry the bananas. Add the sugar and heat, stirring, until the bananas have caramelized. Transfer to a sheet of greaseproof paper and allow to cool.

Spoon the cooled bananas evenly over the caramel in the cake pan.

For the chocolate mousse
Put the gelatine in a bowl of cold water to soften; put the sugar in a saucepan over low heat to melt but don't be tempted to stir it; in a separate saucepan, bring the 240 ml/1 cup cream to the boil over low heat; beat the 560 ml/2⅓ cups cream until soft peaks form.

The sugar will begin to caramelize around the edges. Don't stir it, even now, and when it has turned deep but not dark golden, stir it with a silicone spatula, breaking down any little bits of sugar. Over low heat, slowly and very carefully pour in the boiled cream, in stages. It will bubble up, but this is good. Continue until all the cream has been used up.

In a heatproof bowl, put the chocolate and softened gelatine, squeezed of excess water. Pour the caramel cream into the bowl and mix until melted and smooth. Immediately fold in the whipped cream to create a mousse.

Spoon the mousse into the cake pan to fill the sides and reach the top of the pan. Spread level with a large palette knife and freeze overnight.

The next day, transfer the cake to the fridge to start defrosting.

For the ganache topping
Put the cream, glucose and butter in a saucepan and bring to the boil over low heat. Pour it into a heatproof bowl and add the chocolates. Using a spatula, start to mix in a circular motion, just in the centre of the bowl. Keep mixing in a tight circle until the chocolate starts to melt and emulsify with the liquid. Gradually widen the circle until all the chocolate has melted.

Pour on top of the gâteau. Allow to set before releasing the cake from the pan. Cut into slices using a hot, sharp knife.

A

B

C

Gâteau Saint-Honoré

This is one of the most famous of all French pâtisseries, and it is definitely made to impress. The caramel-tipped pistachios are optional of course, but they add a touch of style – see page 128. It is traditionally made as a large gâteau for the French patron saint of bakers and pastry chefs, Saint Honoré, but I make little individual ones as well.

250 g/9 oz. Pâte Feuilletée (page 16), or storebought puff pastry
½ quantity Pâte à Choux (page 18)
1 egg yolk, to glaze
1 x quantity Crème Diplomate (page 26)
2 tablespoons Grand Marnier liqueur
summer berries, to decorate

Caramel
250 g/1¼ cups sugar
1 tablespoon water

18-cm/7-in. round cake pan (optional)
2 baking sheets, lined with greaseproof paper
piping bag, plain nozzle/tip and star-shaped nozzle/tip
silicone mat (optional)

Serves 6–7

Preheat the oven to 200°C (400°F) Gas 6.

Using a rolling pin, roll out the puff pastry on a lightly floured surface until 6 mm/¼ inch thick.

Lay the cake pan or an 18-cm/7-inch plate on the pastry and cut around it to make a disc. Transfer it to a prepared baking sheet. (Don't throw away the leftover trimmings of pastry – re-roll them, sprinkle grated cheese over them, stamp out rounds and bake to make little cheese puffs. They freeze raw too.)

Fill a piping bag (fitted with a plain nozzle/tip) with the Choux Pastry and pipe a ring around the edge of the pastry circle. Set the piping bag aside for a moment. **(A)**

Brush egg yolk over the ring to give a lovely golden glaze. **(B)**

Using the filled piping bag again, pipe about 7 bulbs onto another prepared baking sheet, about 5 cm/2 inches in diameter and spaced apart as they will expand during baking.

Put both baking sheets in the preheated oven and bake for 10 minutes. Lower the temperature to 180°C (350°F) Gas 4 and leave the oven door ajar ever so slightly to dry the buns out. They won't need that long but the base may need a further 20–25 minutes.

Remove from the oven and transfer the cake base and choux buns to a wire rack to cool.

For the caramel

Put the sugar and water in a saucepan over low heat. Leave it to heat until the sugar has melted and don't be tempted to stir it. Continue

D

E

cooking until it has turned to a golden caramel. Meanwhile, fill your sink with cold water. Once the caramel is ready, it will continue to cook even when it is taken off the heat and you don't want it to brown and burn so dip the base of the pan into the sink of cold water for a few seconds, then set the pan safely on a towel.

Working quickly before the caramel sets, and being very careful not to touch the burning caramel with your fingers, dip the top of each chou bun into the caramel. **(C)**

Set the buns, caramel side down, on a silicone mat or a sheet of greaseproof paper. This will create a neat, flat surface. Allow to cool completely.

Make a hole in the base of each cooled bun with a skewer. It needs to be just big enough to fit the tip of the piping nozzle/tip.

Make the Crème Diplomate following the instructions on page 26, then fold in the Grand Marnier at the end. Fill a piping bag (fitted with a star-shaped nozzle/tip) with two-thirds of the cream. Stick the tip of the nozzle/tip in the hole in each cooled chou bun and fill (do not over-fill!) with cream.

Now pipe shell shapes on top of the choux-pastry ring all the way around the cake. Arrange the filled choux buns on top, caramel side up. **(D)**

Fill another piping bag (fitted with a plain nozzle/tip) with the remaining cream and pipe bulbs in the middle of the cake. **(E)**

Decorate with berries and impress your friends!

To make caramel pistachios for decoration, make a caramel as above using 100 g/½ cup sugar and 2 tablespoons water. Dip the base of the pan into the sink of cold water for a few seconds, then set the pan safely on a towel. **(F)**

Stick a cocktail stick/toothpick into one pistachio at a time and dip it into the caramel. **(G)**

Pull it out of the caramel slowly to form a caramel trail. **(H)**

Allow to set on a sheet of greaseproof paper before pulling the cocktail stick/toothpick out. **(I)**

F

G

H

I

Red berry charlotte

You may be surprised to hear that the 'charlotte' probably originated in England in the late eighteenth century and was named after the wife of King George III, Queen Charlotte. It was the French pastry chef Carême who transformed the cake into what it is today – usually an exterior of light ladyfingers and an interior of vanilla cream or flavoured mousse. You can buy the ladyfingers ready-made of course, but where's the fun in that?!

red berries of your choice
icing/confectioners' sugar, to dust

Ladyfingers
6 eggs, separated
350 g/1¾ cups caster/superfine sugar, plus extra to dust
350 g/2¾ cups plain/all-purpose flour

Raspberry and vanilla mousse
3 leaves of gelatine
250 ml/1 cup whipping cream
125 ml/½ cup Raspberry Purée (page 99)
125 g/½ cup vanilla yogurt
3 tablespoons Cointreau liqueur
1 large egg white
2½ tablespoons caster/superfine sugar

deep, 18-cm/7-in. round springform cake pan
piping bag fitted with a large, plain nozzle/tip

Serves about 8

Start the recipe the day before you want to serve the cake.

For the ladyfingers
Preheat the oven to 180°C (350°F) Gas 4.

Take a sheet of greaseproof paper and place the cake pan on it vertically. Draw parallel lines the same depth as the pan. This will help you make ladyfingers of the right height for the pan. Flip the paper over and place on a baking sheet. On another sheet of paper, draw a circle around the base of the cake pan, flip over and place on a second baking sheet.

Put the egg whites in a stand mixer or in a bowl using an electric whisk and whisk until they form soft peaks. Add the sugar and continue to whisk until well incorporated and glossy. Gradually sift in the flour and fold in with a large metal spoon. Finally, fold in the egg yolks.

Fill the piping bag with the mixture and pipe ovals slightly longer than the depth between the parallel lines on the sheet of paper. You will need about 20 ovals. Sprinkle sugar over them for a lovely crunch.

Pipe or spread the remaining mixture in a disc within the circle on the second baking sheet.

Bake in the preheated oven for 10–12 minutes. Allow to cool completely on a wire rack.

Line a baking sheet with greaseproof paper and place the cake pan on it. Trim the tops and bottoms of the ladyfingers to make them all exactly the same length. Line them up tightly against the inner sides of the cake pan, sugared side out. Trim the baked base to fit and place inside the lined-up ladyfingers.

For the raspberry and vanilla mousse
Put the gelatine in a bowl of cold water to soften; put the cream in a bowl and beat until soft peaks start to form, then refrigerate.

Put the Raspberry Purée in a small saucepan over low heat until hot. Remove from the heat, add the softened gelatine, squeezed of excess water, and stir until it has dissolved. Transfer to a mixing bowl and stir in the yogurt and Cointreau.

Whisk the egg white and sugar as above.

Now line up all 3 bowls. Add a little meringue to the yogurt mixture and beat in with a spatula. Fold in the remaining meringue very gently so as not to knock all the air out. Fold in the whipped cream in the same way.

Allow to cool completely, then spoon into the ladyfinger-lined cake pan, leaving a little gap at the top for the berries. Refrigerate overnight.

The next day, to serve, pile the berries on top. Cut into slices using a hot, sharp knife.

Passionfruit délice

This is a sure showstopper, not only for its appearance, but also for your taste buds. Passionfruit is one of my favourite flavours as it works amazingly well with other ingredients but also stands well on its own. This is a celebration of passionfruit, great for special occasions, but you could make small versions for individual indulgent moments!

½ quantity Almond Cake mixture (page 36) or a 20-cm/8-in. storebought flan base

Passionfruit mousse

3 leaves of gelatine
250 ml/1 cup whipping cream
125 ml/½ cup passionfruit purée
125 g/½ cup passionfruit yogurt
3 tablespoons lime vodka
1 large egg white
2½ tablespoons caster/superfine sugar

Passionfruit jelly

2 leaves of gelatine
100 ml/⅓ cup fresh orange juice
1½ tablespoons sugar
1 vanilla bean, split
100 ml/½ cup passionfruit purée
seeds of 1 passionfruit

Swiss/jelly roll pan, lined with greaseproof paper
deep, 20-cm/8-in. round springform cake pan

Serves 6–8

Start the recipe the day before you want to serve the cake.

Preheat the oven to 190°C (375°F) Gas 5.

Make the Almond Cake mixture following the instructions on page 36. Spread the mixture thinly and evenly into the prepared Swiss/jelly roll pan and bake in the preheated oven for 5–10 minutes. Flip the cake onto a sheet of greaseproof paper dusted with a little semolina. Peel the paper off the top and allow to cool.

Put the round cake pan on the cooled cake and cut around it. Put the cake circle inside the cake pan and set aside.

For the passionfruit mousse

Put the gelatine in a bowl of cold water to soften; put the cream in a bowl and beat until soft peaks start to form, then refrigerate.

Put the passionfruit purée in a small saucepan over low heat until hot. Add the softened gelatine, squeezed of excess water, and stir until it has dissolved. Transfer to a mixing bowl and stir in the yogurt and vodka.

Put the egg white in a stand mixer or in a bowl using an electric whisk and whisk until it forms soft peaks. Add the sugar and continue to whisk until well incorporated and glossy.

Now line up all 3 bowls. Add a little meringue to the yogurt mixture and beat in with a spatula or balloon whisk. Fold in the remaining meringue very gently so as not to knock all the air out. Fold in the whipped cream in the same way.

Allow to cool completely, then spoon into the cake pan on top of the cake base, leaving a little gap at the top for the jelly. Refrigerate overnight.

For the passionfruit jelly

The next day, put the gelatine in a bowl of cold water to soften.

Put the orange juice, sugar and vanilla bean in a saucepan over low heat and bring to the boil. Remove from the heat, add the softened gelatine, squeezed of excess water, and stir until it has dissolved. Transfer to a mixing bowl and stir in the passionfruit purée and seeds. Allow to cool slightly.

Pour the cooled jelly on top of the frozen mousse in the cake pan. Allow to set in the fridge for about 2 hours before releasing the cake from the pan and enjoying this tangy dessert. Cut into slices using a hot, sharp knife.

VARIATION

Add pomegranate seeds to the jelly for an extra splash of colour.

Black Forest gâteau

100 ml/½ cup Kirsch
1 jar of cherry jam
Chocolate Curls (page 33)

Chocolate almond cake
120/½ cup egg whites (about 4 egg whites)
80 g/scant ½ cup sugar
4 eggs
130 g/1¼ cups ground almonds
75 g/scant ⅔ cup icing/ confectioners' sugar
2½ tablespoons plain/ all-purpose flour
2½ tablespoons cocoa powder
2 tablespoons butter, melted and cooled

Kirsch chantilly cream
250 ml/1 cup whipping cream
250 ml/1 cup double/ heavy cream
50 g/¼ cup caster/ superfine sugar
1 vanilla bean

Cherry chocolate ganache
3 tablespoons whipping cream
3 tablespoons Cherry Purée (page 100)
100 g/3½ oz. dark chocolate, chopped
2 teaspoons butter

deep, 20-cm/8-in. round springform cake pan

Serves about 8

Black Forest gâteau originated in Germany, of course, but the cake now has worldwide appeal. Often seen as part of a cake selection in many pâtisseries, the cake got a bad reputation in the 1970s thanks to frozen versions, but I am attempting to bring it back to its rightful place as king of the gâteaux!

For the chocolate almond cake
Preheat the oven to 180°C (350°F) Gas 4.

Put the egg whites and sugar in a stand mixer or in a bowl using an electric whisk and whisk until stiff peaks form.

Whisk in the whole eggs.

Gently fold in the ground almonds, icing/ confectioners' sugar, flour and cocoa powder using a large metal spoon. Finally, stir in the melted butter.

Spoon the mixture into the prepared cake pan and bake for 20–25 minutes or until springy to the touch. Allow to cool in the pan.

For the Kirsch chantilly cream
Put both creams, the sugar and 50 ml/¼ cup of the Kirsch in a stand mixer or in a bowl using an electric whisk. Split the vanilla bean lengthwise using a small, sharp knife and scrape the seeds out into the bowl. Whisk until soft peaks form but don't over-beat otherwise it will go grainy. Refrigerate until needed.

For the cherry chocolate ganache
Put the cream and purée in a saucepan and bring to the boil over low heat.

Pour the boiled cream into a wide, heatproof bowl and add the chocolate and butter. Using a spatula, start to mix the ingredients in a circular motion, just in the centre of the bowl. Keep mixing in a tight circle until the chocolate starts to melt and emulsify with the liquid. Gradually widen the circle until all the chocolate has melted and you have a shiny, smooth ganache. Allow to cool while you assemble the cake – you want it be firmer, like a thick-set cream, but soft enough to spread.

To assemble the cake, cut the cooled cake horizontally into 3 layers using a large, serrated knife. Brush the remaining Kirsch and some cherry jam over 2 of the layers. Top with a good amount of the Kirsch chantilly.

Place one of these topped layers onto a baking sheet lined with greaseproof paper. Top with the second layer. Finally, top with the bare cake layer. Gently press it down with your hand. Spread some jam over it, then some Kirsch chantilly. Using a palette knife, scrape away the excess cream and jam that has oozed out of the side of the cake. Now spread the remaining Kirsch chantilly all over the cake to cover completely.

Freeze for 45 minutes to solidify the chantilly and make it easier to coat in the ganache.

Spread the cherry chocolate ganache all over the cake with the palette knife as neatly as possible. Top with lots of chocolate curls.

Cut into slices using a hot, sharp knife.

Chocolate and cherry pots

These little desserts take the elements of the classic Black Forest gâteau and put them into glasses, something which is becoming increasingly trendy in Parisian pâtisseries – straight-to-table desserts in fancy pots and glasses that will always guarantee the 'ooh' factor.

Chocolate Mousse (page 124, made without gelatine and replacing the 240 ml/1 cup cream with cherry purée)
Chocolate Curls (page 33)

Brownie
50 g/⅓ cup hazelnuts
400 g/14 oz. dark chocolate, chopped
250 g/2 sticks butter
3 eggs
250 g/1¼ cups dark muscovado sugar
100 g/¾ cup self-raising flour
2 tablespoons glacé/candied cherries
2 tablespoons milk chocolate chips

Jelly
2 leaves of gelatine
50 g/2 oz. fresh cherries, plus extra to serve
1½ tablespoons port
2 tablespoons sugar
175 g/6 oz. frozen cherries or berries

Custard
275 g/10 oz. white chocolate, chopped
500 g/2 cups fresh storebought custard
2 teaspoons vanilla bean paste
2 tablespoons Kirsch liqueur

deep, 20 x 30-cm/8 x 12-in. baking pan, greased and lined

Serves 4

Start the recipe the day before you want to serve the cake.

For the brownie
Preheat the oven to 170°C (325°F) Gas 3.

Put the hazelnuts on a baking sheet and roast in the preheated oven for a few minutes, stirring halfway through, until lightly toasted. Leave the oven on. Allow the hazelnuts to cool completely, then finely chop them.

Put the chocolate and butter in a heatproof bowl over a pan of lightly simmering water (not letting the base of the bowl touch the water).

Meanwhile, put the eggs and sugar in a stand mixer or in a bowl using an electric whisk and whisk for about 5 minutes until you can lift up the beaters and leave a figure-of-eight ribbon trail in the mixture.

Stir in the melted chocolate mixture. Sift the flour into the bowl, then add the remaining ingredients. Spoon the mixture into the prepared baking pan and bake in the preheated oven for 25–30 minutes. Allow to cool completely in the pan.

For the jelly
Put the gelatine in a bowl of cold water to soften.

Pit and halve the fresh cherries.

Put the port, sugar and frozen cherries in a saucepan over medium heat and bring to the boil. Remove from the heat and stir in the softened gelatine, squeezed of excess water, until dissolved. Pass the mixture through a sieve/strainer and discard the cherries left behind. Fold in the halved cherries.

Chop the cooled brownie into cubes and divide most of them between 4 serving glasses. Reserve some to decorate. Pour the jelly over the top. Refrigerate to set for 30 minutes.

For the custard
Melt the chocolate on low power in a microwave or in a heatproof bowl over a pan of simmering water (not letting the base of the bowl touch the water).

Fold in the custard, vanilla and Kirsch, then spoon over the set jelly and spread level in the glasses. Refrigerate to set for 1 hour.

Divide the Chocolate Mousse between the glasses and spread level.

Refrigerate overnight to set.

The next day, to serve, top the desserts with the reserved chopped brownie, Chocolate Curls and a fresh cherry.

Chocolate and pear bûche de Noël

½ quantity **Chocolate and Beer Cake (page 163, replacing the beer with pear cider)**
½ quantity **Chocolate Mousse (page 124, replacing half the smaller quantity of cream with pear purée)**

Pear cream
2 leaves of gelatine
100 g/½ cup pear purée
150 ml/⅔ cup double/heavy cream
2 egg yolks
50 g/¼ cup sugar
5 canned pear halves

Pear ganache
50 g/3 tablespoons pear purée
50 g/3 tablespoons double/heavy cream
1 teaspoon ground cinnamon
1 teaspoon mixed spice/apple pie spice
125 g/4 oz. milk chocolate, chopped

2 Swiss/jelly roll pans, lined with greaseproof paper
plain Yule log mould, about 25 x 8 cm/10 x 3 inches, lined with greaseproof paper
sugar thermometer (optional)

Serves 8–10

A bûche de Noël is a Yule log and the traditional French dessert at Christmas. A gutter-shaped mould is filled with cake and mousse among others, and often flavoured with candied chestnuts. I love pear, ginger and chocolate at Christmas so have included all three in my bûche, finished with a spiced pear ganache.

Start the recipe the day before you want to serve the cake. Preheat the oven to 180°C (350°F) Gas 4.

Make the Chocolate and Beer Cake following the instructions on page 163, but replace the beer with pear cider. Spread the mixture evenly into the prepared Swiss/jelly roll pans and bake in the preheated oven for 10–15 minutes. Allow to cool completely, then peel the baking paper off the tops.

Cut one cooled cake to the right size to line the curved Yule log mould, then cut a rectangle from the over cake to seal the length of the mould later. Line the curve of the mould with the first piece of cake. Freeze this and the cake rectangle.

Make the Chocolate Mousse following the instructions on page 124, but replace the smaller quantity of cream with pear purée. Refrigerate to set.

For the pear cream

Put the gelatine in a bowl of cold water to soften; put the purée and cream in a saucepan over low heat and bring to the boil; whisk the egg yolks and sugar in a heatproof bowl until light and fluffy.

Slowly pour the boiled cream into the egg mixture, whisking vigorously. Pour back into the pan and gently heat until the custard thickens or reaches 72°C/162°F on a sugar thermometer. Transfer to a clean bowl and add the softened gelatine, squeeze of excess water. Refrigerate.

Take the Yule log mould out of the freezer and spoon about two-thirds of the Chocolate Mousse into it. Spread level. Freeze for 45–60 minutes.

Take the cake out of the freezer. Cut the pears into quarters and arrange them in a row on the mousse in the Yule log mould. Cover with the pear cream, spread level and freeze for 1 hour.

Remove the cake from the freezer, top with the remaining mousse and cover with the frozen cake rectangle. Press down gently with your hand and scrape off any filling that oozes out. Freeze overnight.

For the pear ganache

The next day, put the pear purée, cream and spices in a saucepan and bring to the boil over low heat. Pour into a heatproof bowl and add the chocolate. Using a spatula, start to mix in a circular motion, just in the centre of the bowl. Keep mixing in a tight circle until the chocolate starts to melt and emulsify with the liquid. Gradually widen the circle until all the chocolate has melted. Allow to cool until firmer, like a thick-set cream, but soft enough to spread.

Remove the cake from the freezer and gently ease it out of the mould and onto a board, flat side down. Spread the ganache over the bûche using a palette knife. Use the palette knife or a fork to create texture on the ganache. Allow to defrost in the fridge and cut into slices using a hot, sharp knife.

Fraisier

The ultimate strawberry and cream cake! This beautiful creation is tricky to get right, but it is always bound to impress. Traditionally made with marzipan on the top, I have simplified mine with a dusting of pistachio sugar which works really well against the bright red of the juicy strawberries.

1 x quantity Almond Cake mixture (page 36, replacing half the ground almonds with ground pistachios)
2½ tablespoons chopped pistachios
250 g/2 cups strawberries
1 x quantity Crème Pâtissière (page 25, adding 50 g/¼ cup pistachio paste [available online or see page 79] to the milk)

Pistachio sugar
100 g/⅔ cup icing/ confectioners' sugar
100 g/⅔ cup pistachios

2 Swiss/jelly roll pans, lined with greaseproof paper
deep, 18-cm/7-in. round springform cake pan
piping bag fitted with a large, plain nozzle/tip

Serves about 8

Preheat the oven to 190°C (375°F) Gas 5.

Spoon the Almond Cake mixture into the prepared Swiss/jelly roll pans and spread level with a spatula. Sprinkle the chopped pistachios evenly over the top.

Bake in the preheated oven for 5–10 minutes or until springy to the touch and golden on top. Flip each slab of cake onto a sheet of greaseproof paper dusted with a little semolina. Peel the baking paper off the top and allow the cakes to cool.

Put the round cake pan on each cooled cake slab and cut around it. Put one cake circle inside the cake pan and set aside.

Cut the stalks off the strawberries in a straight line across the tops. At the same time, try to get all the strawberries roughly the same height; this will make them particularly impressive when you arrange them around the cake. Now halve the strawberries vertically.

Line them up tightly against the inner side of the cake, cut side out, trying to stick them to the pan using the juice of the strawberries. When the pan is lined all the way around, pop the remaining strawberries in the middle of the cake.

Fill the piping bag with chilled Crème Pâtissière and pipe it in and around the strawberries, trying not to dislodge them, as well as in the middle of the cake pan until you reach the top.

Place the remaining cake circle on top and press down gently with your hand.

Refrigerate for about 30 minutes, or overnight if preferred.

For the pistachio sugar
Put sugar and pistachios in a food processor and blend until finely ground.

To serve, dust the fraisier with the pistachio sugar. Cut into slices using a hot, sharp knife.

Sachertorte

- **90 g/3 oz. dark chocolate, chopped**
- **75 g/5 tablespoons butter, softened**
- **3 tablespoons sugar**
- **2½ tablespoons caster/superfine sugar**
- **100 g/scant ½ cup egg whites (about 3 egg whites)**
- **2½ tablespoons plain/all-purpose flour**
- **3 tablespoons cornflour/cornstarch**
- **2 teaspoons cocoa powder**
- **4 tablespoons ground almonds**
- **3 egg yolks**
- **150 g/⅔ cup apricot jam**
- **2 x quantities Ganache Topping (page 124)**

deep, 18-cm/7-in. round springform cake pan, lined with greaseproof paper

Serves about 8

The origins of this Austrian recipe are often disputed but it is still one of the most revered cakes today. This version was devised by the late Professor John Huber who transformed the education of pastry in the UK. He passed the recipe to his protégé and my mentor Yolande Stanley, who passed it to me.

Preheat the oven to 180°C (350°F) Gas 4.

Melt the chocolate on low power in a microwave or in a heatproof bowl over a pan of simmering water (not letting the base of the bowl touch the water). Allow to cool slightly.

Beat the butter and 3 tablespoons sugar together in a stand mixer or in a bowl with an electric whisk until pale and fluffy; whisk together the 2½ tablespoons caster/superfine sugar and the egg whites until stiff peaks form; sift together the flour, cornflour/cornstarch, cocoa powder and ground almonds.

Stir the egg yolks briskly into the melted chocolate, then stir this into the creamed butter. Mix well, then fold in the sifted ingredients with a large metal spoon. Finally, fold in the meringue in 3 stages. Spoon the mixture into the prepared cake pan and bake in the preheated oven for 20 minutes. Allow to cool while you make the Ganache Topping following the instructions on page 124. Now allow the ganache to cool and thicken slightly to a spreadable consistency.

Cut the cooled cake horizontally into 2 layers using a large, serrated knife. Spread half the jam over one layer and put this layer on the base of the cake pan. Top with a little ganache and place the second cake layer on top. Spread the ganache all over the cake with a palette knife. **(A)**

Refrigerate to set for 2 hours or until set.

Place the cake on a wire rack set on a tray. Heat the remaining jam with a splash of water, bring to the boil, then pour over the cake. Refrigerate to set for 1 hour.

Reheat the remaining ganache to soften it and pour it over the cake, spreading if needed. **(B)**

It is traditional to pipe the word 'Sacher' on the cake, to serve. **(C)**

Chilled lemon soufflés

Soufflés are one of the most iconic French desserts and they can take a long time to master. However, this is a simple lemon mousse made in a ramekin and shaped with the help of some greaseproof paper and an elastic band to make it look like a soufflé. What is particularly clever about it is that it is made in advance so you have none of those last-minute nerves about whether your soufflé will rise when your guests are seated at the dinner table! Try the recipe with oranges or grapefruit, too.

4 leaves of gelatine
6 eggs, separated
500 ml/2 cups whipping cream
300 g/1½ cups caster/superfine sugar
grated zest and juice of 4 lemons, plus extra zest to decorate
icing/confectioners' sugar, to dust

4 large ramekins

Makes 4

Start the recipe the day before you want to serve the soufflés.

First prepare the ramekins. Measure the circumference of the ramekins and add 1 cm/½ inch to the figure. Now measure their height and add 5 cm/2 inches to the figure. Take some greaseproof paper and draw 4 rectangles: their length should match that of the recorded circumference; and their height should match that of the recorded height.

Cut out the rectangles of paper and wrap each one around a ramekin. Fasten tightly in place with an elastic band or some sticky tape. Place on a baking sheet and set aside.

Put the gelatine in a bowl of cold water to soften.

Put the egg whites in a stand mixer or in a bowl using an electric whisk and whisk until firm peaks form. Refrigerate while you continue with the recipe.

Put the cream in the stand mixer or in a bowl using an electric whisk again and whisk until soft peaks form. Don't over-beat otherwise it will go stiff and grainy and will look split.

Put the egg yolks and sugar in a heatproof bowl over a pan of simmering water (not letting the base of the bowl touch the water). Whisk with a balloon whisk for 5 minutes or until light and foamy. This is called a 'sabayon'.

Put the lemon zest and juice in a saucepan over medium heat and bring to the boil. Remove from the heat and stir in the softened gelatine, squeezed of excess water.

Add the lemon mixture to the sabayon, whisking quickly until thoroughly combined.

Gently fold the egg whites into the lemon sabayon with a large, metal spoon. When evenly incorporated, fold in the whipped cream in the same way.

Divide the mixture between the ramekins with a spoon – it should reach above the rim of the ramekins by about 3 cm/1¼ inches and be contained by the paper to give you that restaurant 'soufflé' look.

Allow to set in the fridge overnight.

The next day, dust with icing/confectioners' sugar and a little extra lemon zest to serve.

VARIATION

For a hidden little treat, add a couple of raspberries to the base of the ramekin before you spoon in the mixture.

Crêpes Suzette

When my sister and I were kids, once Christmas was over we couldn't wait for Pancake Day in February. We always had sugar and lemon on them and – don't judge me too harshly – whipped cream in a can! One year when we had no lemons in the house, we used oranges instead and I fell in love with this new pancake filling. Classic Crêpes Suzette is served in so many restaurants and is a good example of guéridon service where a waiter performs a piece of culinary theatre directly at the customers' table, for example when making the Suzette sauce and flambéeing the Grand Marnier in front of the customers!

Crêpes
100 g/¾ cup plain/ all-purpose flour
2 eggs
about 200 ml/¾ cup milk
a pinch of salt
a pinch of sugar
2 tablespoons butter

Suzette sauce
50 g/¼ cup sugar
juice of 2 oranges
Candied Orange (page 33)
peeled segments of 2 oranges
a dash of Grand Marnier liqueur

Makes 4–6

For the crêpes

Put the flour in a mixing bowl and make a well in the middle. Add the eggs to the well and start incorporating the flour into the eggs using a balloon whisk.

Now start adding milk, a little at a time, and whisk it in until you have added about 200 ml/ ¾ cup and you have a smooth, creamy batter. Whisk in the salt and sugar. Allow to rest for about 30 minutes.

Melt the butter in a frying pan, or a pancake pan if you have one, over medium heat. When it has melted, pour away the excess into a bowl and reserve for later. Pour a ladle of batter into the hot pan and tilt the pan to spread the batter evenly over the base – you want nice, thin pancakes so don't pour in too much batter at once. Allow to cook for 1–2 minutes, then check the underneath by lifting up the edge of the pancake with a spatula. If the underneath looks golden and cooked, flip the pancake over and cook for about 1 minute until the other side is golden too.

Keep the pancakes warm in a low oven, separated by pieces of greaseproof paper. If the pan is getting too dry, add some of the reserved melted butter.

Continue making pancakes until you have used up all the batter.

For the Suzette sauce

Put the sugar in a frying pan over medium heat until it melts and starts to caramelize. Meanwhile, warm up the orange juice.

Carefully add the warm orange juice to the frying pan, stir and heat until combined with the caramelized sugar.

Add the Candied Orange and orange segments to the pan. Remove the pan from the heat and carefully add the Grand Marnier. Shake the pan a little over the heat and stand back slightly. The steam from the pan will ignite and the alcohol will burn off – this is perfectly normal.

Put the pan back on the heat and add the pancakes, one by one. Fold each one in quarters with the help of a spatula and douse in the sauce before transferring to a warm plate and repeating with the remaining pancakes.

Accompany with vanilla ice cream, if you like!

Tarte Tatin

This popular apple tart was allegedly created by accident at the Hotel Tatin in Lamotte-Beuvron, France, around the 1880s. The owner, Stéphanie Tatin, overcooked the apples for a pie and when she realized that they were close to burning, she put some pastry on top and baked it anyway. When she served it, it was immediately loved and the tarte Tatin was born.

6 medium apples, eg 3 Cox and 3 Granny Smith
200 g/1 cup sugar
50 g/3 tablespoons butter
a pinch of salt
a dash of Calvados liqueur
200 g/7 oz. Pâte Feuilletée (page 16), or storebought puff pastry

ovenproof, 20-cm/8-in. frying pan

Serves 4–6

Preheat the oven to 200°C (400°F) Gas 6.

Peel and halve the apples, remove the core, then cut into large wedges or quarters. Refrigerate until needed.

Put the sugar in the ovenproof frying pan over low heat to melt it. It will begin to caramelize around the edges. Don't stir it, and when it has turned amber, stir it with a silicone spatula, breaking down any little bits of sugar.

Add the butter, salt and Calvados, stir until melted, then remove from the heat and allow to cool slightly.

After a few minutes, the caramel will have started to set. Now arrange the apple wedges in the pan, curved side down. Be careful not to touch the caramel with your fingers. **(A)**

Using a rolling pin, roll out the puff pastry on a lightly floured surface until slightly larger than the frying pan. Cut it into a circle the size of the pan. Lay it over the apples in the pan and tuck it in between the apples and the edge of the pan. **(B)**

Prick the pastry in a couple of places with a fork and bake in the preheated oven for about 30 minutes or until golden brown.

Remove from the oven and allow to cool for 2–3 minutes. Put your serving dish on top of the pan and holding everything with oven gloves or a towel, VERY CAREFULLY (the caramel will be boiling hot and WILL leak out) flip the pan over so that the plate is underneath. **(C)**

Set the plate and pan down, then gently pull the pan away. **(D)**

Serve with the caramelized juices and vanilla ice cream, if you like.

Crèmes brûlées

I love crème brûlée! On my first trip to Paris we had a lovely family meal in a restaurant and for afters we had this crunchy custard in a terracotta pot. I was instantly hooked and it is still one of my favourite things – rich, creamy vanilla custard topped with crisp caramel. In honour of my parents, for this photograph, I used ramekins that were given to them as a wedding gift. The crème brûlée's origins have long been disputed between France, Spain and England. All three countries have different varieties and all claim to have invented it. France has the brûlée, Spain has crema catalana and we have Trinity cream that was invented in the 1800s in Cambridge. I don't mind who invented it – it's up there with the best sweet treats!

600 ml/2⅔ cups double/heavy cream
1 vanilla bean, split
6 egg yolks
100 g/½ cup sugar, plus 2 tablespoons, to dust
1 teaspoon icing/confectioners' sugar

4 large ramekins
kitchen blowtorch (optional)

Makes 4

Preheat the oven to 150°C (300°F) Gas 2.

Put the cream and vanilla bean in a saucepan over low heat and bring to the boil.

Meanwhile, put the egg yolks and sugar in a mixing bowl and whisk with a balloon whisk until light and fluffy.

Slowly pour the boiled cream into the egg mixture, whisking vigorously until evenly incorporated.

Pass the mixture through a fine sieve/strainer and discard the vanilla bean and any bits of egg shell that may have accidentally crept in!

Divide the custard mixture between the ramekins and place them in a deep roasting pan. Pour water into the pan to reach halfway up the sides of the ramekins. This is called a 'bain marie' and will ensure that the crème brûlées bake evenly and gently.

Bake in the preheated oven for 40–45 minutes. There should still be a slight wobble in the middle of the crème brûlées when you shake them gently.

Remove the crème brûlées from the oven, take them out of the roasting pan and allow to cool completely. You can then refrigerate them until needed, if you like.

When you are ready to serve them, dust the 2 tablespoons sugar over them, followed by the icing/confectioners' sugar. The sugar will give you crunch and the icing/confectioners' sugar will give you shine.

You can now blast the tops of the crème brûlées using a kitchen blowtorch, or place them under a hot grill/broiler. When they are ready, they should be a deep orange-brown.

Allow to cool slightly before serving. The caramel will have set and you will have the pleasure of that delicious cracking noise!

Apple and Calvados croissant butter pudding

I hate throwing away food, especially the croissants we haven't managed to eat on Sunday mornings! So if this happens, I put them in a pan with some custard and make a bread and butter pudding. The French have something resembling this with stale bread and a custard sauce (wonderfully entitled 'pain perdu', ie. 'lost bread') but it is closer to French toast as it is fried. I like adding apples because they give such a wonderful texture and flavour but you could try it with pear and ginger instead. This also works really well with Italian pannetone at Christmas time.

500 ml/2 cups milk
500 ml/2 cups double/ heavy cream
1 vanilla bean, split
1 cinnamon stick
3 star anise
2 tablespoons Calvados
3 eggs
3 egg yolks
200 g/1 cup sugar
2 croissants, stale but not too stale
2 tablespoons butter, melted
2 Braeburn apples
2 tablespoons semi-dried apples, chopped

large pie dish or baking pan, well greased

Serves 4–6

Preheat the oven to 200°C (400°F) Gas 6.

Put the milk, cream, vanilla, cinnamon, star anise and Calvados in a saucepan over medium heat and bring to the boil.

Put the whole eggs, egg yolks and sugar in a stand mixer or in a mixing bowl using an electric whisk and whisk until pale and fluffy.

Slowly pour the boiled cream into the egg mixture, whisking vigorously until evenly incorporated.

Pass the mixture through a fine sieve/strainer and discard the vanilla bean, cinnamon stick, star anise and any bits of egg shell that may have accidentally crept in!

Halve the croissants horizontally and brush the melted butter over them. Arrange them in the prepared pie dish or baking pan.

Halve, core and roughly chop the fresh apples. Scatter these and the semi-dried apples over the croissants in the pan, then pour the custard in over the top.

Using a spatula, press down the croissants so that they start to soak up some of the lovely custard mixture.

Bake in the preheated oven for 25 minutes. It should still be a little runny in the middle.

Serve with vanilla ice cream, or just some whipped cream flavoured with a little lemon and vanilla extract.

29
BOULANGERIE

Consider those types of bakery treats that aren't quite desserts, gâteaux or pâtisserie, but likewise aren't quite bread or cookies. Brioche (made with an enriched yeast dough), croissants and basic cakes all fall in this category, as do puff-pastry products. You might have these for afternoon tea or for a lazy Sunday breakfast when you have friends staying with you. They are quietly satisfying but still feel like something special to be savoured. Particularly good are the variations you can make once you've got the hang of croissant pastry – pains au chocolat, pains aux raisins and almond croissants, all of which will make you never want to buy ready-made again.

Bakery and viennoiserie

Spiced ginger and honey cake

In the autumn there is nothing better than a slice of spicy, dense ginger cake and a cup of tea. This is a really warming cake that works just as well with chopped candied chestnuts in place of the ginger towards the end of the year. I use preserved ginger and honey in mine as well as a medley of spices to lift the humble cake to new heights. You will find something similar in French homes called 'pain d'épices'. Delicious!

100 g/7 tablespoons butter
100 g/½ cup dark muscovado sugar
2 tablespoons golden or corn syrup
75 g/¼ cup honey
100 g/⅓ cup black treacle/dark molasses
grated zest of 1 orange
150 g/⅔ cup self-raising flour
2 teaspoons ground ginger
1 teaspoon mixed spice/apple pie spice
1 teaspoon ground cinnamon
½ teaspoon ground star anise
½ teaspoon ground cloves
3 balls of preserved ginger, finely chopped (reserve the syrup)
2 eggs
5 tablespoons milk

Glaze
3 tablespoons apricot jam
1½ tablespoons honey

1-kg/2-lb loaf pan, lined with greaseproof paper

Serves 6–8

Preheat the oven to 160°C (325°F) Gas 3.

Put the butter, sugar, syrup, honey, treacle/molasses and orange zest in a saucepan over medium heat and cook until melted. Stir well, then remove from the heat and allow to cool slightly while you continue with the recipe.

Sift the flour into a mixing bowl and add the ground ginger, mixed spice/apple pie spice, cinnamon, star anise and cloves and two-thirds of the chopped ginger. Mix together.

Add the cooled melted mixture, followed by the eggs and milk. Mix thoroughly with a wooden spoon.

Spoon the mixture into the prepared loaf pan and bake in the preheated oven for about 1 hour. The cake should be risen and deep golden brown.

For the glaze

Put the jam, 2 tablespoons of the reserved ginger syrup, the honey and remaining chopped preserved ginger in a saucepan over low heat. Heat gently until it starts to bubble. Set aside until the cake has baked. It can be warmed up later if necessary.

Remove the baked cake from the oven, carefully tip it out of the pan and set it on a wire rack. Pour the hot glaze over it and serve warm.

Prune and Armagnac cake

I love to make this brownie-type cake at Christmas as a lovely alternative to something more traditional. It goes well with all sorts of accompaniments, such as ice cream, brandy crème anglaise or simply a dollop of cream. Lots of people have traditions of soaking fruit at Christmas to give as gifts, and the prunes soaked in Armagnac for this cake would fit the bill. For the cake, the longer you soak the prunes before using, the better the flavour.

250 g/9 oz. dark chocolate, chopped
200 g/14 tablespoons salted butter
5 eggs, separated
100 g/½ cup raw cane sugar
75 g/⅔ cup plain/all-purpose flour
75 g/¾ cup ground almonds
cocoa powder, to dust

Soaked prunes
3 tablespoons Armagnac brandy
grated zest of 1 orange
1 teaspoon ground cinnamon
1 teaspoon mixed spice/apple pie spice
½ teaspoon ground nutmeg
a pinch of ground cloves
130 g/1 scant cup soft, pitted prunes

deep, 20-cm/8-in. round cake pan, lined with greaseproof paper

Serves 6

Start the recipe the day before you want to bake the cake.

For the soaked prunes

It is best to start soaking the prunes at least 1 day in advance of baking the cake, or if possible, soak them several weeks in advance in a sterilized jar. Their flavour will improve immeasurably over time.

Put the Armagnac, orange zest, cinnamon, mixed spice/apple pie spice, nutmeg and cloves in a saucepan and bring to the boil.

Put the prunes in a heatproof bowl, pour the hot soaking liquid over them and allow to cool completely. Cover the bowl with clingfilm/plastic wrap and allow to soak overnight.

The next day, preheat the oven to 180°C (350°F) Gas 4.

Put the chocolate and butter in a heatproof bowl over a pan of simmering water (not letting the base of the bowl touch the water). Stir occasionally until melted, then remove from the heat.

Put the egg whites and 1 tablespoon of the sugar in a stand mixer or in a bowl using an electric whisk and whisk until it forms stiff peaks.

Meanwhile, put the egg yolks and the remaining sugar in the stand mixer or bowl using an electric whisk and whisk for about 5 minutes until you can lift up the beaters and leave a figure-of-eight ribbon trail in the mixture.

Stir in the melted chocolate mixture.

Put the soaked prunes in a food processor and process to a purée. Add them to the egg and sugar mixture and stir well.

Fold the flour and almonds into the mixture with a large, metal spoon.

Finally, fold in the egg whites very gently in 3 stages so as not to knock all the air out.

Spoon the mixture into the prepared cake pan and bake in the preheated oven for about 30–40 minutes.

Allow to cool in the pan, then dust with cocoa powder just before serving.

Brioche

For me, brioche is the king of breads. First recorded in France in the fifteenth century, it has been a favourite of royalty through the ages. This wonderful enriched bread goes with so many things, from tangy lemon curd to creamy pâté, from indulgent chocolate ganache to silky soups. It is infinitely versatile. If you have stale brioche left over, use it instead of croissants in the Apple and Calvados Croissant Butter Pudding on page 153.

500 g/4 cups strong white bread flour
50 g/¼ cup sugar
15 g/1 cake fresh yeast or 7.5 g/ 3 teaspoons dried yeast
a generous pinch of salt
6 large eggs
250 g/2 sticks butter, softened
1 egg, lightly beaten, to glaze

1-kg/2-lb. brioche pan or loaf pan, greased and dusted with flour

Makes a large brioche

Put the flour and sugar either in a mixing bowl with a wooden spoon, or in a stand mixer with a dough hook. Add the yeast on one side of the bowl and the salt on the other side. You want to keep them apart for now, as yeast is a living organism and the salt will kill it if it comes into direct contact with it.

Add the eggs and mix until everything comes together into a dough.

Transfer the dough to a lightly floured surface and knead with your hands until it starts to come together. It will feel very wet and messy to start with but this is good. Don't be tempted to wash your hands or simply to give up – just keep going.

When the dough starts to come away from the work surface and seem less sticky, add a little piece of butter and knead it in. (You can do this by hand, or transfer the dough back to the stand mixer.) Keep adding one little piece of butter at a time and kneading it in until all the butter has been used up and the dough is silky and elastic.

Cover the bowl with clingfilm/plastic wrap (making sure there is enough height in the bowl so that the rising dough won't touch and get stuck to the clingfilm/plastic wrap). Allow to rest somewhere warm for 12–14 hours. An airing cupboard would be perfect for this.

Remove the risen dough from the bowl and shape it into a ball. Place it in the prepared brioche or loaf pan.

Allow to rise, uncovered, for 2 hours.

Just before you are ready to bake the brioche, preheat the oven to 190°C (375°F) Gas 5.

Brush the beaten egg over the brioche to glaze it. Bake in the preheated oven for 10 minutes, then lower the oven temperature to 180°C (350°F) Gas 4 and bake for 20–30 minutes. When it is crusty and golden, remove the brioche from the oven and tip it out of the pan (be careful as it will be very, very hot). Give the base a little tap and if it sounds hollow, it is ready.

Allow to cool slightly before eating, but bear in mind that brioche straight out of the oven is amazing! Serve simply with butter and maybe a sprinkling of sea salt – divine.

Chocolate and beer cake

This has to be one of my favourite chocolate cake recipes, not just because it contains two of my greatest loves – chocolate and beer – but because it is so easy it is to make and yet it is incredibly tasty and moist. It is based on an American Cola cake that a family friend once made for me when I was a kid so I adapted it to make it quirkier and it came out so well. It also works extremely well with French cider or a good ale. I think you will be truly surprised at just how great this cake is.

125 g/1 stick salted butter
125 ml/½ cup lager such as Stella Artois
125 g/1 cup self-raising flour
10 g/⅓ cup cocoa powder
½ teaspoon bicarbonate of soda/baking soda
125 g/⅔ cups sugar
75 ml/⅓ cup milk
1 egg, beaten
1 teaspoon vanilla extract
50 g/1½ oz. dark chocolate, broken into pieces

1-kg/2-lb loaf pan, lined with greaseproof paper

Serves 6–8

Preheat the oven to 180°C (350°F) Gas 4.

Put the butter and beer in a saucepan over low heat and heat until the butter has melted.

Sift together the flour, cocoa powder and bicarbonate of soda/baking soda in a mixing bowl and add the sugar, milk, egg, vanilla, chocolate pieces and melted butter mixture.

Spoon the mixture into the prepared loaf pan and bake in the preheated oven for 50 minutes. A skewer inserted in the middle of the cake should come out clean and the top of the cake should bounce back slightly when prodded.

Allow to cool slightly in the pan, then tip out and serve warm as a dessert with a chocolate sauce, or eat cold when it becomes moist and irresistible.

VARIATION

Top the cooled cake with Ganache (page 30).

Raspberry and pistachio financiers

These moist little bakes make perfect petits fours but also work very well as dessert canapés for parties. The added bonus here is that the method for making them is so simple and involves no creaming or whisking – just melting, mixing and baking. In my book, pistachio and raspberry are a marriage made in heaven but you could put your own twist on them by substituting pear and hazelnut and some extra spices thrown in for some Christmas cheer! I made these in mini loaf pans but you can buy excellent silicone financier moulds online to give you that real Parisian feel.

60 g/4 tablespoons butter
1 teaspoon vanilla extract
110 g/¾ cup icing/ confectioners' sugar
3 tablespoons ground almonds
2½ tablespoons pistachios
40 g/⅓ cup plain/ all-purpose flour
1 teaspoon baking powder
2 egg whites
2 teaspoons honey
25 g/¼ cup frozen raspberries

Topping
50 g/scant ½ cup icing/confectioners' sugar
juice of 1 lemon
25 g/3 tablespoons pistachios, chopped

8–10 mini loaf pans

Makes 8–10

Preheat the oven to 170°C (325°F) Gas 3.

Put the butter and vanilla in a saucepan over medium heat and allow to melt. Continue to cook until it turns golden brown – this is called a 'beurre noisette', ie butter the colour of nuts. It gives financiers their deep golden colour. When the butter has turned the right colour and stopped sizzling, it is ready. Remove from the heat and allow it to cool completely.

Put the icing/confectioners' sugar, ground almonds, pistachios, flour and baking powder in a food processor and process until finely ground. Transfer to a mixing bowl.

Put the egg whites and honey in a stand mixer or in a bowl using an electric whisk and whisk until soft peaks form.

Fold the meringue into the mixing bowl with a large, metal spoon, then fold in the cooled beurre noisette.

Divide the mixture between the prepared loaf pans but don't fill them too much because they rise quite a lot. Place some frozen raspberries on top and bake in the preheated oven for 15–20 minutes.

For the topping
Whisk together the sugar and lemon juice with a fork or balloon whisk to make a glaze.

Spread it over the baked financiers and top with chopped pistachios.

These financiers are lovely with a cup of tea or a strong, robust coffee.

Palmiers

Made using puff pastry, palmiers are delightful little cookies that can be sweet or savoury. Also known as elephant ears, they are often made using the puff pastry left over after making other pastries such as millefeuilles (pages 55 and 56). You can make little ones or large ones, but I particularly like them small so I can dip them in my espresso on a Sunday morning. I don't do this every week, but when I do, it's a real treat!

175 g/6 oz. Pâte Feuilletée (page 16), or storebought puff pastry
2 tablespoons sugar
¼ teaspoon ground cinnamon

baking sheet, greased

Makes 12

Preheat the oven to 200°C (400°F) Gas 6.

Using a rolling pin, roll out the puff pastry on a lightly floured surface until about 5 mm/¼ inch thick. Cut out a neat rectangle, 24 x 14 cm/ 9½ x 5½ inches using a small, sharp knife.

Mix together the sugar and cinnamon and sprinkle three-quarters of it over the pastry.

Starting from one short end, roll up the pastry until you reach the middle, then roll up the other short end until you reach the middle. Trim the ends neatly, then cut into slices 1 cm/½ inch thick.

Arrange the slices, cut side up, on the prepared baking sheet. Reshape them gently if they look squashed.

Sprinkle the remaining cinnamon sugar over them and bake in the preheated oven for about 12 minutes, until puffed and golden.

Transfer to a wire rack to cool completely.

VARIATIONS

Chocolate: add 25 g/1 oz. grated chocolate to the cinnamon sugar. When they come out of the oven, grate a little more chocolate over the top.

Cherry and almond: add 25 g/1 oz. chopped glacé/candied cherries and 1 tablespoon finely chopped almonds to the cinnamon sugar.

Christmas: replace the cinnamon sugar with 25 g/1 oz. chopped mincemeat and ½ teaspoon mixed spice/apple pie spice, ½ teaspoon ground cloves and ½ teaspoon cinnamon. When they come out of the oven, dust some icing/ confectioners' sugar over the top.

Wild mushroom and thyme: replace the cinnamon sugar with 25 g/1 oz. chopped dried wild mushrooms and 1 teaspoon fresh chopped thyme.

Cherry tomato and Parmesan: roast 25 g/ 1 oz. cherry tomatoes in a low oven until dry and crispy. Blitz in a food processor with 3 teaspoons grated Parmesan and add to the pastry in place of the cinnamon sugar.

Plum Pithiviers

This was the first piece of pastry-work my Grandad ever made when he was doing his training. It is so straightforward – two discs of puff pastry filled with sweet frangipane – and I love to add plums, too. They can be sweet or savoury and are often made as one large tart. I remember making about 1,000 little wild mushroom and thyme ones last year for a function in Wales! Be warned that they can take a bit of time to make perfectly, but they always wow people.

1 x quantity Frangipane (page 29)
375 g/13 oz. Pâte Feuilletée (page 16), or storebought puff pastry
150 g/5 oz. plums
100 g/scant ½ cup plum jam
1 teaspoon mixed spice/apple pie spice
1 egg, lightly beaten, to glaze

round cookie cutters, about 10 cm/4 in. and 12 cm/5 in. in diameter
baking sheet, lined with greaseproof paper
piping bag fitted with a plain nozzle/tip

Makes 4–6

Make the Frangipane following the instructions on page 29, then refrigerate to set while you continue with the recipe.

Pit and quarter the plums. Put the plums and jam in a saucepan over medium heat and warm just until the plums are beginning to cook and break down. Do not be tempted to cook it for too long as you still want some texture in there. Allow to cool slightly.

Using a rolling pin, roll out the puff pastry on a lightly floured surface until about 7 mm/⅓ inch thick. Stamp out 4–6 rounds using the smaller cookie cutter, and the same number using the larger cookie cutter. Arrange the rounds on the prepared baking sheet.

Spoon or pipe a little of the frangipane onto the smaller pastry rounds. These will be the bases of the Pithiviers. Leave a 1-cm/½-inch border around the edge. You need to reserve the same amount of frangipane for later.

Put a teaspoonful of the cooled plum compote onto the frangipane. Now top with the remaining frangipane so that the blob of compote is encased in frangipane.

Place the larger rounds of pastry on top of the frangipane and seal by pressing the tines of a fork around the edges.

To make the distinctive pattern on the pastry tops, take a very sharp knife and score curved lines on them, from the middle to the edge, all the way around.

Brush the beaten egg over the Pithiviers to glaze them. Bake in the preheated oven for 20 minutes or until puffed up and golden.

Viennoiserie

Croissant pastry is the basis of so many universally popular breakfast viennoiserie. Whether you treat yourself to a pain au chocolat on a Sunday morning, or pick up a naughty pain aux raisins on the way to work, it always brightens up a morning. And when you have mastered the technique of making the pastry on pages 20–23, you can create your own treats to rival anything you can buy ready-made!

Praline pains au chocolat

Make the Croissant Pastry following the instructions on page 21 until you have made the third turn.

Melt 100 g/½ cup praline paste (available online) and 100 g/3½ oz. chopped dark chocolate together in a heatproof bowl over a pan of simmering water.

Spread it over a sheet of greaseproof paper with a spatula until about 5 mm/¼ inch thick. Alow to set completely.

Cut the hardened praline into strips about 5 mm/¼ inch wide. You can snap them to the right length later.

Roll the croissant dough out on a lightly floured surface into a rectangle about 3 mm/⅛ inch thick. Cut it into strips about 11 cm/4½ inches wide for a regular-sized croissant. Lay 1–2 strips of the praline across one short end of the dough, Snap the praline to the right length. Now roll up the dough completely and place, seam side down, on a lined baking sheet. Flatten the pastry slightly with your hand.

Rise and bake as described on page 22.

Pains aux raisins

Make the Croissant Pastry following the instructions on page 21 until you have made the third turn.

Roll the dough out on a lightly floured surface into a rectangle about 3 mm/⅛ inch thick. Scatter 1 teaspoon ground cinnamon, 2 tablespoons raisins and 2 tablespoons sultanas/golden raisins evenly over the dough.

Roll up the rectangle from one long side, as you would for a Swiss roll/Jelly roll. Cut into 2-cm/1-inch slices and arrange them, cut side up, on a lined baking sheet. Reshape them gently if they look squashed.

Rise and bake as described on page 22.

Almond and marzipan croissants

Make the croissants following the instructions on pages 20–23, but insert short, thin strips of marzipan (if you can get Brandy marzipan, that works really well) in the base of the croissants before you roll them up. Roll them up and sprinkle flaked/slivered almonds on top before rising and baking as described on page 22.

Index

D

E

F

G

H

WILL TORRENT is a leading UK pastry and chocolate expert, boasting an award-winning pâtisserie background. His career started at the age of 16 working for Heston Blumenthal at the world-renowned The Fat Duck. He has won numerous awards, including Young Chef of the Year in 2009 and the WorldSkills UK Outstanding Achievement Award in 2012. Will has collaborated with top chefs such as Jamie Oliver and James Martin, and his experience includes working for prestigious establishments like The Dorchester and Claridges. He is a familiar face on television, with appearances on BBC's *Sweet Baby James*, *Ready Steady Cook*, *The Apprentice*, Channel 4's *Sunday Brunch* and ITV's *This Morning*. Currently, Will serves as a Senior Development Chef at Waitrose. His expertise is highly valued in the industry, evidenced by his roles as a judge for the Great Taste Awards, Academy of Chocolate Awards, Quality Food Awards, RACA Annual Awards of Excellence, World Marmalade Awards, International Salon Culinaire, and as the host of the Craft Guild of Chefs National Chef of the Year. He is also a member of the Royal Academy of Culinary Arts and the Craft Guild of Chefs.

JONATHAN GREGSON is an award-winning food and travel photographer based in London. His work appears in *Waitrose Food*, *Tatler*, *Lonely Planet Magazine*, *The Guardian* and *The Sunday Times*, among others. His work has taken him to far-flung destinations such as Brazil, Rwanda, Libya and Mauritius. For Ryland Peters & Small he has also photographed *Salt* and *The Perfect Start to Your Day*.

Acknowledgments

Wow, what a journey.

Big thanks to Bea Vo for introducing me to RPS. To Cindy, Leslie, Megan, Julia and Céline and the rest of the team: what can I say other than I must have been an absolute nightmare but hey, we got there and thank you for your amazing belief and support for me. Massive thanks to the 'words cannot explain' beauty of Jonathan Gregson's photography. JG you really know how to shoot them don't you – 'Ooh, hello'. To the talented Liz Belton for the props, and the fantastic, supportive food stylists and assistants who helped me put the book together: Rosie Reynolds, Emily Kydd and Kathryn Morrissey – you are all stars and I couldn't have done it without you. Not forgetting my buddy Alistair Birt – this guy is a star and is going places!

To Brian, Gary and Fiona – thank you for the amazing quotes for this book. You have all played such key parts in my career and I am honoured to have you as colleagues and friends!

Where would I be without Heston Blumenthal?! Heston, thank you so much for that week, a little over 10 years ago, and for changing my life! That week truly did set my heart on being the best and striving for excellence in everything I do. Thank you also for the amazing and humbling foreword to this book – it means such a lot.

Massive thanks to Jamie Oliver, who over the last few months has been incredibly supportive and awesome. I know you don't often give quotes for books, so to have your name on the front of my book means so much. I grew up watching you on TV and thinking, as soon as The Naked Chef aired, 'I want to be like him!' – happy days.

To my lecturers at Thames Valley University (now UWL): Prof David Foskett MBE and his team who taught me – thank you for your support and knowledge. The team at Bachmanns and to all those who have helped train me both at university and in the industry – a serious thank you!

Which of course brings me on to Yolande Stanley MCA. Without her, I wouldn't be writing this book. I owe her everything! Yolande took me under her wing and moulded me into the pastry chef I am today. She has been there every step of the way and I could not have done any of it without her. Yolande, you really are a rock! Thank you for believing in me and for being a truly great friend.

To the entire team at Waitrose – you really are amazing. I'm so proud to be part of the best Innovations Team in the industry. Thank you for your ongoing support. To the amazing guys in the kitchen: Jonathan, Paul, Martin, Neil, James, Kathryn, Heather and those who we've worked with before – you guys are the best! Enormous thanks to Paul and Suzanne Walker and to Neil Nugent for giving me the chance.

Enormous thanks to Martin John and the team at Kenwood for helping us out with the beautiful Kenwood equipment and the guys at The Pampered Chef for giving us the great equipment and baking needs. Exciting times ahead… To Ross Sneddon, big thanks for your help and support.

To my amazing team at Freedom Management: Darrin, Martyn, Graham, Keith and Nick – I don't know what I would do without you. What a journey we are on and who knows what's going to happen next. You guys really are brilliant! With a massive thanks to Steve and Carey Baynes for their support and introductions.

To all of my amazing friends – there are just too many of you to mention by name. You mean so much to me and I could not have got to this point without your love, support and friendship, so thank you from the bottom of my heart. You know who you are.

My amazing grandparents: Nans and Pops, Granny and Grandad. You truly are my inspiration, not only from a food point of view, but as a child when you taught me to work hard and reap the benefits. Just incredible people.

Mum, Dad and Sophie – thank you for everything. You are amazing. Love you lots.

And finally to JC – you really are a Superstar.

R

S

T

V

W

Y

WILL TORRENT is a leading UK pastry and chocolate expert, boasting an award-winning pâtisserie background. His career started at the age of 16 working for Heston Blumenthal at the world-renowned The Fat Duck. He has won numerous awards, including Young Chef of the Year in 2009 and the WorldSkills UK Outstanding Achievement Award in 2012. Will has collaborated with top chefs such as Jamie Oliver and James Martin, and his experience includes working for prestigious establishments like The Dorchester and Claridges. He is a familiar face on television, with appearances on BBC's *Sweet Baby James*, *Ready Steady Cook*, *The Apprentice*, Channel 4's *Sunday Brunch* and ITV's *This Morning*. Currently, Will serves as a Senior Development Chef at Waitrose. His expertise is highly valued in the industry, evidenced by his roles as a judge for the Great Taste Awards, Academy of Chocolate Awards, Quality Food Awards, RACA Annual Awards of Excellence, World Marmalade Awards, International Salon Culinaire, and as the host of the Craft Guild of Chefs National Chef of the Year. He is also a member of the Royal Academy of Culinary Arts and the Craft Guild of Chefs.

JONATHAN GREGSON is an award-winning food and travel photographer based in London. His work appears in *Waitrose Food*, *Tatler*, *Lonely Planet Magazine*, *The Guardian* and *The Sunday Times*, among others. His work has taken him to far-flung destinations such as Brazil, Rwanda, Libya and Mauritius. For Ryland Peters & Small he has also photographed *Salt* and *The Perfect Start to Your Day*.